THE SOCIAL BASIS
OF THE GERMAN
REFORMATION

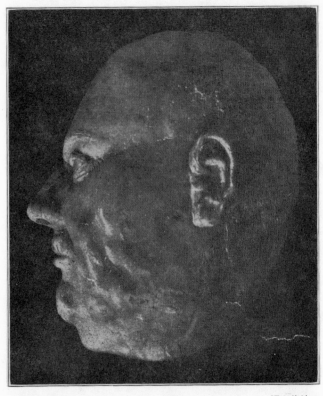

PHOTOGRAPH OF A WAX-MODEL TAKEN FROM LUTHER'S
DEATH-MASK

(From Benkard, *Das ewige Antlitz*.   English edition, *Undying Faces*,
Hogarth Press, London.)

THE SOCIAL BASIS

OF THE GERMAN

REFORMATION

MARTIN LUTHER AND HIS TIMES

BY

ROY PASCAL

[1933]

AUGUSTUS M. KELLEY · PUBLISHERS

NEW YORK 1971

First Edition 1933

(London: Watts & Company, *5 & 6 Johnson's Court, Fleet
Street E. C. 4,* 1933)

Reprinted 1971 by
AUGUSTUS M. KELLEY · PUBLISHERS
REPRINTS OF ECONOMIC CLASSICS
New York   New York   10001

By Arrangement With The Author

I S B N 0 678 00549 4

L C N 68 30539

PRINTED IN THE UNITED STATES OF AMERICA
by SENTRY PRESS, NEW YORK, N. Y. 10019

FOREWORD

MARTIN LUTHER is known to posterity chiefly as a theologian who disrupted the medieval Church. The vast majority of the books written about him wage over again the battle he fought against the papacy. But when he made his onslaught on the Catholic Church he was not opposing a mere set of dogmas, nor even mere ecclesiastical practices. The Catholic Church was in his time a political institution of immense size and power, existing side by side with the secular powers proper. Its theology bore within itself the sanction of its existence as a secular power. Any attack on the assumptions of the Church's theology was bound to be an attack on the Church as an institution; and such an attack could not be made in isolation, but was bound to affect profoundly the whole structure of society. When, then, Luther advocated the idea of a spiritual in place of the old temporal Church, he had in mind, clearly or indistinctly, a new organisation of society. Thus it was no accident that he was called on to take a leading part in the social and political struggles which followed on his theological controversies. And he

v

never doubted that it was his task, his calling, to define the principles of the new political order which crystallised out in Germany between 1518 and 1555. Indeed, in the decisive struggles which brought forth the new order—that of princely absolutism—Luther played the part of a protagonist, defining the new relationships between Church and State, between the German princes and the Emperor, between subjects and ruler.

In the light of this all-embracing activity of Luther, the venerable controversy as to whether he was divinely or diabolically inspired seems irrelevant. Great difficulties have been caused in the past through the inconsistencies of much of his theory. Lutherans have excused them on the plea that Luther did not quite understand the bearing of some of the statements he made; Catholics have eagerly pointed out their contradictoriness.[1] Similarly with many of the practical results of his doctrines which were in some respects opposed to his original teaching, and in general showed that this champion of freedom of conscience laid the theoretical bases of a period of oppression, in the realm of thought as of politics. In spite of the apologetics of Lutherans, Luther himself always confirmed what he effected, and was not aware of any fundamental contradictions in his teachings. And this cannot be explained

[1] For a short account of these contradictions see my article in the *Hibbert Journal* for July 1931.

away on the grounds of his naivety, since he showed himself so able and far-sighted in practically all that he did. The essential fact of his theoretical and practical activity is that, while it cannot be fitted into any logical system, yet Luther himself always felt that he was acting consequently. And he did not act in isolation, capriciously, but was always followed by a great and powerful body of opinion.

Starting from this fact, it has been my aim in this book to find the principle guiding Luther's thought and the political developments attendant on it. It is therefore an *interpretative* study of Luther, viewing his work in connexion with the social and political developments of the time. With Luther it is clearer than with most thinkers that his age would be unthinkable without him. Modern research reveals more and more indisputably that he would be unthinkable without his age. But of course " the age " cannot be referred to as if it were a simple entity. Society was then in rapid movement. It was composite of a number of groups, of classes with definite interests and definite moral and metaphysical codes, warring amongst each other for the hegemony of society. This war was carried on in every sphere, in metaphysics as in practical life. It is fundamental to the understanding of Luther to see him as belonging to one of these groups, leading and guiding its struggle. Thus, to understand him

FOREWORD

we have to understand the complexion of society at
that time, and in particular the principles of the
group of which Luther was a member, which produced the type of thought to which Luther adhered.
We do not expect these principles to be logical,
deduced from some absolute truth. But we do
expect them to be consequent, since they were the
conditions of existence of a powerful class, associated
on a real basis of community of interest. It is this
consistency, the logic of a social class, which this
book attempts to trace beneath all the apparent
inconsistencies of Luther's activity. It is not, then,
a mere history of Martin Luther who produced a
new religious principle, but attempts to define Luther
as the leader of a class which formed one of the main
factors in the breakdown of the medieval system in
Germany and constituted the basis of a new society.

CONTENTS

ix

CHAPTER I

PRE-CONDITIONS FOR LUTHER'S REFORM

THE reformation which Martin Luther inaugurated and cemented is part of a general crystallisation of social forces into a new social structure. It stands at the dawn of what is called the modern era, which is variously described, according to its various aspects, as scientific, individualistic, capitalistic, bourgeois, constitutional, and so on. This fact, then—that the religious reformation is accompanied by a number of parallel reformations—is enough to make it imperative that any study of Luther should constantly refer to general conditions at those times. But Luther himself, though claiming to be essentially a theological reformer, was willy-nilly brought to pronounce decisions of far-reaching importance on many social questions of the time, became as it were the mouthpiece of the new form of society, and produced the ethical sanctions of its acts. Indeed, Luther takes up as big a place in social history as in theological or ecclesiastical; and a true estimate of the importance of his rôle in ecclesiastical history can be gained only by a recognition of his place in social history. One must go further: only such a study can give a clear insight into the nature of his theological

reform and determine the co-ordinates of his standpoint. It will be seen that the question of the truth
or falseness of Luther's theology will not be broached,
it being outside the sphere of the historian. It is
necessary to construct a unified, harmonious plan
of the actions of Luther, the great man, the leader,
eliminating by one's point of view the glaring contradictions invented by his co-believers and his enemies,
discovering in his mental constitution a purposeful-
ness equivalent to that of which he felt himself
possessed. What, then, were the characteristics of
the time into which he was born?

By 1500 the Holy Roman Empire of the German
nation was an anachronism. The Emperor was
without power and authority except by virtue of his
private possessions. Very rarely did any proposed
measure touch members of the Imperial Diet closely
enough to ensure effective common action under
imperial lead. ·The distinction between the interests
of the individual princes and the imperial policy was
always evident—even war against the invading Turk
was not always felt as a common cause. When
general levies were voted by the Diet, they were
contributed dilatorily, or perhaps not at all, with a
general distrust of their administration. The Emperor Maximilian himself, in whose interest it was
to see that contributions were made punctually and
strictly according to the decisions of the Diet, would
not enforce them in his own hereditary lands for
fear of rousing discontent and turbulence. The
Imperial Court of Law (*Reichsgericht*) was held in

little esteem. Owing to the Emperor's impe-
cuniosity, its judges and assessors were badly and
irregularly paid and its meetings infrequent. And
the Emperor was not strong enough to carry out its
decrees if action was needed against any of the more
powerful princes. During the fifteenth century
anarchy was rife; and many Germans, still attached
to the idea of a united Germany, and aware of the
inadequacy of their organisation when compared
with that of centralised France or England, set their
thoughts to reforming the constitution of Germany.

The Cardinal Nicolas of Cusa was the chief theo-
retician of political reform. He saw that the
interests of the Empire and the princes could be
reconciled only by giving the princes a greater share
in government. His proposed system took out of the
hands of the Emperor the exercise of justice, both
the appointment of judges and the execution of
decrees; it provided for regular sessions of the Diet,
and for equable and regular taxes by which the
administration could be supported. The greatest
practical steps in this direction were taken at and
immediately after the election of Maximilian as
King of the Romans. Maximilian was weak in his
private possessions; at the moment of his election
he was about to undertake a burdensome war which
would tax his resources to the uttermost. The
electors made him king and heir to the Empire for
this very reason: they promised him help in his war
in return for promises on his part that he would
grant them reforms of the imperial constitution—

reforms such as Cusanus had contemplated. Some of these promises were carried out, though from the very beginning of Maximilian's reign he showed himself opposed to sharing the executive power with the electors. Through the energy and determination of the ecclesiastical Prince Berthold of Mainz some points were realised. Maximilian, continually warring, was forced to give way here and there; he had to grant a reform of the Imperial Court of Law, and to allow the Diet to form a committee of government to take his place during his absence in the field. And both these reforms became permanent, though under Maximilian they were effective only in a small degree, owing to his continual interference and irresponsibility. But this Emperor was not only romantically imbued with medieval ideals of empire; he saw, too, that the strength of his greatest rival, the King of France, lay in his absolutism. When he had the power he repudiated his reforms and responsibilities, and Germany relapsed again into the state of anarchy of the fifteenth century— though the growing preponderance of the territorial princes organised this anarchy to some extent and divided the land into two camps. At the end of the fifteenth century the princes had shown the way to the Emperor by the organisation of the Swabian League, instituted to put into effect the decisions of the Diet—" a magnificent representation of the idea of empire," as Ranke calls it; the organisation of the princes into Catholic and Protestant leagues after the breakdown of the attempts at reform shows the same self-consciousness, the same aim of self-preservation among the princes, and a realisation that their interests and those of the Emperor were incompatible, that the ideal of unity of the Empire was meaningless. It is characteristic of the aims of the bargaining parties that both neglected to give to the imperial cities any adequate representation in the Diet, though they were financially the most important element of the Empire.

These times see, then, a new grouping among the secular powers. Through aggrandisement and internal organisation the interests of the territorial princes become clearer; nationalism, the solution in Spain, France, and England, is in Germany replaced by particularism—though enthusiasm for the Empire is widely retained as a sentiment used chiefly for polemical purposes. Accompanying this new grouping a new attitude towards the Church becomes articulate. From the fourteenth century onwards the papal Church developed more and more clearly its financial organisation. Its constitution became more centralised and its financial demands more frequent and burdensome. In England, Spain, and France this development was countered by the rise of a national Church (cf. Wiclif); and strong rulers could occasionally refuse to pay papal dues. In Germany no such drastic opposition was possible, but many of its elements were present. Many of the princes gained privileges, which were assured to them by concordats; they sometimes refused to pay the extraordinary tithes demanded by the popes;

they protested against the high and recurrent charges of annates. The national bishops themselves often refused to carry out completely the policy of Rome. They were themselves burdened with dues payable to Rome, and did not further campaigns for collecting money for purely papal ends, *e.g.*, for the building of St. Peter's, for crusades. They were jealous of their own authority in their dioceses; Pfefferkorn, for instance, the papal agent in the attempted oppression of the Jews at the beginning of the sixteenth century, received more hindrance than support from the Archbishop of Mainz, in whose diocese he was working.

This discontent with the domination of the Church found expression in the philosophy of the times. The sentiment of nationalism developed. This was due also to the rivalry of other secular powers, of course, such as France—many writers devoted learned tomes to proving the superiority of the German nation over the French; but the great mass of nationalistic work was written against the Church as the foreign exploiter of the people of Germany. There was a popular hatred of Churchmen, particularly prelates, because of their Italian ways; and there grew up the fiction of the " good old times," of the noble, unspoiled Teuton, which gained credence even among humanists who were devoted to classical culture. Like this nationalistic sentiment, a new morality, or revived morality, was put to the service of anti-clericalism. The sense of responsibility in the higher clergy towards their flock was at this time—under the pontificate of an Alexander VI, a Julius II, a Leo X—very weak, and their conduct laid itself open to criticism. The opposition between the profession of priesthood and the conduct of priests made such criticism all the more justifiable. But there is no doubt that the mass of moral polemic directed against the priesthood was out of proportion, both according to its quantity and its virulence, to the moral state of the clergy. There was no such virulent polemic against the manners in the secular courts; and there were, too, vigorous reform movements in the Church itself—as, for instance, in the religious order to which Luther himself belonged—besides numerous examples of enlightened piety amongst the prelates of the Church. Most of this antagonism towards the clergy was inspired by national and local feeling against the drain of money from Germany to Rome.

Ecclesiasticism was sapped in yet another way. For long there had been a movement in theology to break down the medieval entity of the Church-State, and to distinguish sharply between the sphere of divine and natural law. Questions were being more and more divided into religious and secular, and the latter freed from interference from the former. It was a sign, as Troeltsch has remarked, of the growing power of the secular bodies, the principalities, and townships.[1] Thus many of the

[1] Ernst Troeltsch, *Soziallehren der christlichen Kirchen*. Tuebingen, 1912.

revolts against the secular powers during the later
Middle Ages were evangelical, pietistic, aiming at
a return to the unity of the Church-State, where all
matters should be settled according to religious
principle. The Papacy itself accepted this division
of divine and natural law by claiming that the order
of the Church should be governed by its own rational
law, it being the earthly representation of Christ;
but its opponents and the supporters of the secular
powers called the priesthood merely the spiritual
aspect of humanity, and disputed its right to earthly
titles and honours. By this definition of the Church
not only had it no right to earthly possessions, but
also the secular powers were entirely freed from
the control of Christian morality—the keen logic of
Calvin was brought by this thought momentarily to
a conception of the evolution of forms of society,
which permitted of no permanently valid morality.[1]

These movements in the conceptions of Empire
and Church were accompanied by what has been
widely held to be a revolution in philosophy and art.
Enough has now been written on this subject to show
that the " Renaissance " was no new phenomenon,
but was slowly prepared for during the Middle
Ages; [2] conditions were now ripe for the complete
emergence and popularisation of values which had
long been pushing to the surface. Humanism stood
essentially for the secularisation of morals; but while

[1] Cf. H. Hauser, Les débuts du capitalisme, ed. 1931, pp. 49 ff.
[2] Cf. among others the work of Burdach, Reformation und
Humanismus in Italien und Deutschland.

it was anti-clerical, it was not anti-Christian, and in only very rare cases anti-religious. Some humanists, it is true, went so far as to doubt the literal truth of the Bible, but almost without exception they considered it to be a divine allegory and to contain, in allegorical form, divine wisdom. And the sayings of Christ were for them the summit of wisdom, especially those relating to human behaviour.

The effect of their attitude was to liberate men from the rule of the Church. Morality, they said, did not consist in submissively following the dictates of others, however authoritative these others might be, but in a free, rational approval of one's acts. They remained Christian—though generally without subscribing to the Church's creed and without participating in its rites—because their reason could construct no better morality than the Christian; but they laid the accent on the self-determination of the individual more than on the rightness of his views. This makes it clear why they so admired the ancients and why they were continually accused of " epicureanism "; for, for the Stoics and Epicureans, their favourite philosophers, the power of self-determination was an unchallenged axiom, and the idea of the good life was limited completely to this world.

This turning from a teleological conception of the world to a rational has generally been looked on as a purely philosophical development. There is no place here to analyse the conditions of the emergence of humanism; but it is sufficient to point out that

9

its development is parallel with the general political development of the times. The individualisation and secularisation of thought, of morals, are adequate to the self-assertion of the secular powers. And their dependence on the political forces comes to light exactly where contradictions can be discovered in their thought and actions. Very few of them —Valla, the Italian humanist, is the outstanding exception—attacked the *idea* of a priesthood, of a hierarchy in the Church, although their ethics, logically applied to society, would have done away with the Church altogether. They considered an authoritative control over morals necessary for the people, as did the secular powers; their criticism of the Church, while aiming at a purification of the morals of the priesthood, as far as the form of the Church was concerned helped mainly to destroy the Church as a secular, financial body. The vast majority of the humanists, when confronted with Luther's reformation, supported it enthusiastically so long as it was theological and moral, but drew back in horror when it seemed that Luther was destroying ecclesiasticism completely and really liberating consciences. Their moral attitude was determined by a body of interests which they repre-sented; indeed the general characteristic of those times was the emergence of moral systems corres-ponding to the interests of the various secular bodies. That which the humanists represented—on the whole the patrician, hereditary, " aristocratic " middle-class in the Free Towns—was partly revolutionary, partly conservative; there could be here no question of an abstractly constructed morality; a phrase which is, in any case, meaningless. A second main anomaly in their thought was their patriotism. Here again there are exceptions—Erasmus is a prominent one; but it seems unaccountable that a body of men who were not only rationalists but also worshippers of classical culture should have been so often such ardent patriots. It is perhaps understandable in the Italian humanists, who considered themselves the direct heirs of Rome; but why a Wimpheling, a Reuchlin, and all the rest, should have so praised their country can be explained only by their having being led in all their thought by certain concrete interests, which could in the main well use rationalism, but needed also obscurantism. So wilful a distortion of facts in the service of so dishonourable a passion as hatred of another nation, as we see in works like Wimpheling's *Germania*, are reliable signposts to the origin of humanistic ethics, which made possible its loftiness and imposed on it basic restrictions.

So far the period round 1500 has been defined roughly as the battleground between the developing secular powers and the Church as a secular power. Within the secular powers themselves, however, there were a number of conflicting elements; and the temporary solution of these antitheses completed the structure of the epoch. The commercial and colonial enterprise of the later Middle Ages had given rise to a strongly organised moneyed class;

and with the development of the papacy as a financial power with vast reserves there grew up a class of bankers which created a new and mighty body of interest in Europe. Developing first in Italy, the chief colonising country of the Middle Ages and the domicile of the Popes, these financiers exerted influence over most of Europe, at times controlling the customs, and consequently the tariff policy, at other times the fiscal policy, of many countries and communities, even of great Powers such as France and England. By 1500 the Italian banking houses were rivalled, if not eclipsed, by financial businesses in Germany, which were able to develop in the free imperial cities, and which worked out further the principles of finance, profiting by the experience of the Italian houses and the historical situation. Many of these financiers had a meteoric career, but the principles they represented were constant, and exerted a consistent influence on the trend of political and social development.

By 1500 the potentialities of capital were already clear and a considerable differentiation between the various kinds of capital already was existent. This differentiation between commercial, industrial, and banking capital became rapidly sharper during the first half of the sixteenth century, there being a marked tendency towards neglecting the former two in favour of the last; many historians and moralists of the time noted this with regret, and attributed the growing impoverishment of the age to the turning of capital from productive enterprise to financial speculation and dealing in bills of exchange. Banking capital was at first, so far as Germany is concerned, associated with commerce, and particularly with the precious East Indian trade. The cargoes arriving at Antwerp offered an evident opportunity for speculation and for monopoly. With bad communications and varying regulations in the various international fairs, dealing in bills of exchange also gave easy profit to an international organisation. But in commercial transactions there is always an element of risk. The financiers, particularly those with large reserves, soon found that interest-bearing loans to municipalities and principalities were the safest, as generally the most lucrative, form of investment. In the stress of war, princes, kings, and emperors were ready to give high interest on short-term loans, and the securities they could offer were of incalculable value to the capitalists. Thus the Fugger, at the beginning of their greatness, took possession of the copper mines of Tirol as forfeited securities, which enabled them to monopolise the copper market; and by introducing capitalistic methods of production in other mines put into their hands they increased the value of these pledges many times over.

The aim of such financiers was to make political powers dependent on their loans; and consequently they often controlled politics. By granting or withholding loans they decided on victory or defeat, on peace or war. Particularly was this so in the troubled and anarchical state of Europe in the first

13

years of the sixteenth century, when there was a great shifting of alliances and no definite alignment of inimical forces, and when they were able to give loans to either of the warring sides at their will. With the advent of the Emperor Charles V, however, and with the development of the Lyons fair as a French financial camp pitched over against Antwerp, the Emperor's headquarters, a new situation crystallised out. A check was thereby put on the international activities of the bankers; and while they could still demand high interest, and still, by granting or refusing loans, determine at different points the immediate course of history—as, for instance, Anton Fugger's refusal to grant Charles V a loan in 1527, which meant that the imperial army sacked Rome in lieu of pay—yet they became tied to one or other of the warring parties, bound up with the interests either of the Empire or of France.[1] Charles used Antwerp as his private bank, while Francis of France used Lyons in the same way; and there were repeated impeachments for high treason against the financiers in both places, with consequent confiscation of goods and forced loans. Both Charles and Francis were politically strong enough to threaten to repudiate debts, and as their financial position deteriorated with the long wars, they both resorted to a more and more dictatorial attitude towards the bankers. At one moment all the German financial houses in Lyons—who were, of

[1] A detailed account of the economic and political activities of the banking class is to be found in R. Ehrenberg, *Capital and Finance in the Age of the Renaissance*.

course, not at all identified with the interests of the German Empire—were closed by order of the King, and the bankers could prove their loyalty only by granting fresh loans on the increasingly dubious security of Francis and his successors. The case of the Fugger is typical. Having determined themselves as bankers of the Emperor, both of Maximilian and of his successor Charles, whose election their money decided, there was no means for them to break their connection with the imperial house. It brought them vast possessions of great value. They were given the revenue of the three great ecclesiastical orders of knights in Spain, where they worked mines, particularly of quicksilver, of great value. Concessions were given them in Naples. But they could not do business with any of Charles' enemies: they could not even retire from business, though it seems that from about 1530 onwards they wished to liquidate their affairs. They were forced over and over again to rescue Charles from his financial difficulties, unwilling, in spite of the high rate of interest offered, to accept the securities or concessions he gave in return. They used up their own credit in supplying him with money. They, in common with all other financiers of the times, became the pawns of the politically strong princes, and when they were exhausted, a general bankruptcy was declared by the Kings of France and Spain; and public opinion, the opinion of all nationalists, condemned them as the cause of the ruin of princes. They were tools in the strengthening of absolutism, but were destroyed as dangerous as soon as absolutism was firm enough to stand without them.

Commercial capital was also a force which could be used by the secular princes, having at the same time elements of danger for them. Rings of merchants were formed, generally at ports, especially at Antwerp, who monopolised trade in certain goods, particularly in Eastern products.[1] Their artifices have been brilliantly described by Luther. They controlled prices and supply, and ruined the small traders. So long as the Prince was powerful enough, or if he controlled the source of production, he could take a share in these monopoly profits —Luther complains that the Princes had so often a finger in the merchants' pie that they would not reform the injustice of monopoly. But if the Prince was weak, or so far removed from the centres of production or distribution as to be at the mercy of merchants, not his own subjects, he had from it only loss to himself and his land, where the existence of the petty trading class was threatened. The usual nationalist defence in such cases—the monopolisation of such commerce by the Prince within his boundaries by means of a tariff-wall—contributed to the increase in the cost of living which was so noticeable at that time; but this policy was supported by the petty middle-class traders and producers

---

[1] The question of legislating against monopolies arose at the Diet of Cologne, 1512, and repeatedly in the period following. At the Diet of Nürnberg, 1522, legislation restricting monopolies was passed, but did not affect them seriously. See Schapiro, *Social Reform and the Reformation*, pp. 37–39.

because it ensured their existence and threw most of the burden on to the lower classes and the peasants.

This differentiation between middle class and lower class—artisans and peasantry—was advanced too by the rôle of industrial capital. The existence of capital made it possible for one master to control several workers,[1] and it had long been common for one merchant to control production and price over large areas. Industries on a larger scale became possible through the division of labour and the consequent development of machines; notably in the paper-making, printing, mining, and metallurgical industries, machines led to concentration of production and to the beginnings of a specific proletariat which could defend its interests only by striking. But not merely in this way was a working, non-possessive class created. The craft-guilds, where the struggle between masters and journeymen had always existed, found themselves threatened in their very existence by the methods of individual capitalists, and the masters sought to assure themselves by gaining complete control over the constitution of the guilds, exercising a monopoly in the various localities, and making the attainment of mastership difficult to all but their personal heirs.[2] A class of

[1] At Schwarz in Tirol, for instance, the number of mine-masters fell from thirty-one in 1470 to six in 1530, with a corresponding increase in the size of the undertakings. Mechanisation of the mining industry was greatly advanced by the use of hydraulic power.

[2] K. Lamprecht in *Zum Verständnis der wirtschaftlichen und sozialen Wandlungen in Deutschland vom 14ten zum 16ten Jahrhundert*, has described this process of the proletarisation of journeymen.

hereditary masters grew up—the patriciate of the cities, and its supporters—and a class of hereditary subordinate workers; and though, through the later Middle Ages, many edicts were published to remedy this tendency, by the sixteenth century it had become a recognised system. It had the effect of uniting, up to a certain point, the interests of the journeymen and the peasants; for, while all town organisation was to the detriment of the latter through price-control, urban legislation was now in the hands of a hereditary class of owners, and struck equally against artisans and land-workers. It was also the policy of many cities to refuse civic rights to the peasants who constantly flocked to the towns, and thus a real class of non-possessors was created. In the economic crisis of the sixteenth century these lower classes were, indeed, hit hardest, for while there was a great increase in the prices of industrial products, the price of agricultural produce and wages increased more slowly, often only at the cost of a struggle. With the exploitation of the journeymen there was joined a sort of colonial policy towards the peasants. Thus in the peasant wars of this century we find the proletariat involved on the side of the peasants.

By 1500, then, the balance of power of the Middle Ages, such as it had been, had completely broken down, and had split up into a number of antagonistic interests, all of which were self-conscious enough to make a sharp clash of policy inevitable. No longer was the structure of Europe the outcome of the solution of the antithesis between Pope and Emperor.

of the poorer boys, gained part of his living by singing. The teaching at the school was mainly grammatical and formal, and though he distinguished himself by his intellect and his skill in writing Latin, he spoke later in life in harsh terms of the hardness and aridity of his schooldays.

In 1501 he matriculated at the University of Erfurt. There he studied the scholastic philosophers, learned their terminology, and puzzled over their problems. The course consisted chiefly in the study of logic and dialectic, with a little formal rhetoric, based on Aristotle; and to this was added a mass of questions and answers in the natural sciences, in astronomy and physics, without system or principle, and without experimental examination. Later Luther expressed himself thus on the subject of this education: " I had to read the devil's muck, the philosophers and the sophists, with great expense, labour, and harm to myself, so that I have enough to do to sweep it all away." At the same time, other influences were moving in the University. Erfurt was one of the most active centres of humanistic thought. Under the leadership of Mutianus, who lived close by at Gotha, the classics were tended and eloquence studied. Several notable classical scholars were contemporaries of Luther's there— amongst others Crotus Rubeanus, the part author of the *Epistolæ obscurorum virorum*; Johann Lang, who read Greek; Spalatin, who was an accomplished Latin scholar. Luther himself learnt to esteem the authors of antiquity, and though his Latin was never

23

elegant, he often quoted aptly from classical authors. He read Ovid and Vergil with pleasure, authors not favoured by the schoolmen. Little, however, is known of his student life except that he had the reputation of brooding over philosophical problems, and learned to play the lute, finding in music a great solace. In 1505 he became Magister, and should have proceeded to the legal profession.

But at this decisive moment his natural piety was exalted by two chance occurrences which changed his plans. The sudden death of a friend and the terrors of a thunderstorm produced a turmoil in his mind which he could allay only by vowing to take holy orders and enter a monastery. In spite of the looseness of life amongst some of the clergy, the earnestness and idealism of many priests with whom he had come into contact had impressed him, and gave him the hope that by adopting their mode of life he could get rid of the burden of sin of which he was acutely conscious. He became a novice at a monastery which belonged to the congregation of Observants, a society of reform within the Augustine order which laid great stress on strict individual discipline and asceticism. In spite of the remonstrances of his father, who was deeply disappointed at his decision to leave a career which promised so much honour, and of his friends, to whom the difficulties and temptations of the monastic life were not unknown, he proceeded in 1507 to the priesthood. His passionate preoccupation was to save his soul, and this period of preparation seems to have been remarkable for the agony which the consciousness of sin produced in him. He was repeatedly assailed by " devils," and in his anguish was subject to fits of a peculiar nature. The General Vicar of the Augustine Congregation in Electoral Saxony, Johann Staupitz, a man distinguished for his wisdom and earnestness, took particular notice of the novice who was so deeply troubled by his faith. The advice he gave was admirable: he told Luther to abate his self-torment and to give himself over in all humility to faith in Christ's sacrifice. Luther, however, was absorbed in his problems and anguish, and went to extremes of self-mortification in order to satisfy his conscience. Later he bitterly attacked the whole system of disciplinary penance and mortification, and inveighed scornfully against the monkish belief in their efficacy; but he himself had in his youth an exaggerated belief in self-chastisement which was not general among his associates; and Staupitz found it necessary to warn him not to conjure up imaginary sins and indulge in the feeling of sinfulness, for this was itself sinful pride.

Luther began in the monastery his theological education proper, but found its formalism as arid and repugnant as the philosophy of the University. He acquired, however, considerable proficiency in the painstaking dialectical methods of scholasticism, and the first commentaries we have of his are, formally, completely in the scholastic tradition. He devoted much time to the study of the Vulgate, and Staupitz, seeing his ardent interest in the Bible,

decided he should specialise in a study of the Holy
Scriptures and the biblical commentators. In 1508
he was sent to the University of Wittenberg, there to
complete his theological studies and to take his
doctorate. Here, too, he found scholastic philosophy
and theology dominant, though the University was
a secular, not an ecclesiastical, foundation, having
been founded some years previously by the Elector
Frederick the Wise of Saxony. Troubles in his
Congregation necessitated his recall from Wittenberg
before he could take his doctorate, and he busied
himself for some time subsequently with monasterial
affairs, taking part in controversies, lecturing.
By this time he was a man of some responsibility
in his Congregation, but his commentaries and
glosses are of little distinction. In a few matters he
shows the influence of modern thought; he examines
and compares texts with a critical eye, he spends
time studying Greek and Hebrew (though attaining
proficiency in neither), and he deals out hard words
to the " sophists " who had more faith in their logic
than in the words of Holy Scripture. He told later
how he found a copy of the works of the heretic
Huss in the library of the monastery. He opened it,
and was horrified to find there pure Gospel teaching.
He put the book away, however, obediently, con-
soling himself with the thought that what he had
read must have been written before Huss fell into sin.

The troubles in his Order which were the cause of
his recall from Wittenberg were due to Staupitz'
desire to apply the reformed discipline of the Con-

gregation of Observants to all Saxon monasteries of the Order. This plan was opposed by seven priories of the Congregation, which alleged that the value of the reform lay in its providing a distinction between ordinary standards and their own. Luther stood with the Congregation against Staupitz; and in 1510–1511 he was sent as delegate of the Congregation to Rome to plead their point of view before the Procurator of the Order. The mission was unsuccessful in its appeal, but a compromise was proposed which won over Luther to the side of Staupitz, and made his transference from Erfurt advisable. On the whole, Rome did not make any deep impression on him. He noted many things—the sobriety of the Italians, the clean and well-appointed hospitals, the excellent organisation of charity. He was struck by the immoral and scandalous talk. But on this visit to the sacred city he did not go in a frame of mind which would permit of free criticism; and he accomplished all the usual exercises of the pilgrim. In Milan on the return journey he attended a celebration of the Eucharist in the Ambrosian form, which had been forbidden by a papal ruling—a lesson he would not forget.

On his return from Italy Luther again took up his studies at Wittenberg, and proceeded in 1512 to his doctorate. From this time he lived mainly in Wittenberg, being attached to an Augustine monastery there, lecturing and preaching; from 1516 he preached publicly and in German. In 1512 he became sub-prior of his adopted monastery; and

in 1516 he was made District Vicar of his Order,
holding office immediately under Staupitz. One
of the duties of this office was to get personally into
touch with the monks of the Order and to guide
their consciences. In this Luther excelled. He
showed himself sympathetic, generous, firm, and to
the prestige of his office added esteem for his person,
so that he became a personage of great weight and
consideration in Saxony. He came into touch with
the chief intellectual figures and events of the times.
The humanistic principle of the return to original
documents guided his own search for truth, so that
he rejected the authority of the medieval commentators on the Bible, and called for a return to the
original documents of Christianity. His opinion
was demanded in the Reuchlin quarrel, in which he
sided with the partisans of free inquiry against the
intolerant dogmatism of the scholastic theologians;
he wrote to Erasmus assuring him of his sympathy,
but reproving him for not insisting sufficiently on
the primal necessity of divine grace; he showed
that he approved in general of the theme of the
Epistolæ obscurorum virorum,[1] though censuring their
frivolity. Through his friend Spalatin, who was
tutor and preacher at the Court of the Elector of
Saxony, he was in constant touch with his prince,
though he actually never met Frederick the Wise.

These years from 1512 onwards see Luther's
entrance into the public life of his times. The

[1] A very blunt satire of the manners and methods of thought
of the theologians of the time.

anguish of his self-torments grew less as he grew more absorbed in positive problems and realised his responsibility towards society. In this period fall, too, the first indications of his future heresy. The earliest records of his thought show him to have been full of scorn for the arid, patchwork logic of the late schoolmen. After 1512 he carefully studied the greater theologians of the late Middle Ages, in particular Occam and Biel, and by 1515 was ready to reject their system itself. That is, he did not reject all their doctrine. He accepted much of their teaching concerning penance and rites, on the relationship of natural and divine law, of temporal and ecclesiastical authority, of reason and revelation, and on other points. But on the central doctrine of grace and sin, and on the method of gaining salvation, he found their teaching erroneous. Grace was for Occam not a positive substance, but a " spiritual ornament," signifying the lack of sinfulness. Forgiveness of sin was not, then, an addition to the soul, but merely the non-imputation of sin. Biel and Occam believed, too, that man has power in himself to attain this grace. By changing his heart, by eliminating the will to sin, he can cause a change of heart in God, attract God's grace. For Luther, however, the central theological fact was the passionate consciousness of his sinfulness and of his powerlessness to earn grace. He demanded the certainty of salvation. The non-imputation of sin was only a first step; the crown must be the gift of a positive substance, grace, which would transform the soul. Thus he insisted, in distinction to Occam, on the need in the process of salvation of a positive irrational element. At the same time, he could not accept the theory of the German mystics whom he studied equally carefully. For Tauler and the unknown author of the *Theologia Germanica* God was the All and the All-Good, and the task of man was unification with this All of which he was a fragment. The method for them was the annihilation of the individual through contemplation and ecstasy. But in Luther's experience evil as well as good had a definite individuality, and man's will, after the Fall, was evil; there was no human means of reconciling the two opposites. Though open to the seductions of the state of bliss the mystics describe, the state of perfect union with God, Luther could not believe that it could be permanent, that there could be a permanent solution of the antithesis God—man.[1] And while the mystics, in their extreme devotion to God as the All-Good, were ready to accept even eternal damnation, Luther demanded the certainty of salvation.

Aristotle, the philosopher of the School, was, for the rationalism of his metaphysics and the secularity of his ethics, the main antagonist for Luther; and Augustine was his master among the theologians, though it cannot be claimed that he understood Augustine. In 1515–1516, in the lectures on Paul's

---

[1] In 1525 Luther wrote (*De servo arbitrio*, Vol. XVIII): " The human will is as a beast ridden by the devil or by God, and which goes whither the one or the other will."

Epistle to the Romans, Luther came to a first formulation of his own doctrine. References to Saint Paul had been frequent in his earlier commentaries and lectures, and it is significant that while he insisted, in a truly revolutionary way, on ignoring the medieval theologians and on returning to the first documents of Christianity, he chose as his main authority the first great metaphysician of the Christian Church, the man who made of the doctrines of Christ a system and a church. The statement of Romans i. 17 was the starting-point of his theology; how could he gain this faith which would so completely justify the believer? In these lectures of 1515 he only lays the foundation of his answer. He says: God's nature is entirely different from ours, His whole plan and being are beyond our comprehension, we cannot hope to understand His righteousness; we have no right therefore to expect that earthly righteousness will ensure our justification in God's eyes, and it is of no use our straining every nerve to attain earthly holiness; all good works, from mere monastic exercises to the most fruitful self-sacrifice, are of no account before God. All we can do is to throw ourselves on Christ's mercy and believe in Him, to act and suffer in faith. Further than this Luther did not at this time go. He isolated faith from the Church, made it a matter for the individual only, but did not discuss the nature of salvation except in so far as he said that it was impossible to earn it. The counterpart of his theology could be seen in his frequent criticism of those who believed in the efficacy of ecclesiastical exercises. Luther already poured his scorn on sinners who hoped to gain salvation by observing the ordinances of the Church, and combated the idea of a heavenly reward for good deeds—in this he was supported by a great number of moralists, both ecclesiastical and secular, who were striving for the victory of the true doctrine of Christ.

Luther's theology was completed in the *Commentary on the Epistle to the Romans*, 1517,[1] and the *Commentary on the Epistle to the Galatians*,[2] finished a little later. In the first stage of his doctrine, in which he conceived of man as a powerless tool in God's hands, a sinful creature without merit or deserts, whose salvation depended on the incomprehensible justice of God, the only possible attitude for man was absolute resignation to the will of God. But a sudden light came to show him the way out from this dark, pessimistic resignation. Pondering the nature of God's righteousness, the solution flashed on him, lying hid in his favourite texts—" For therein is the righteousness of God revealed from faith to faith: as it is written, the just shall live by faith " (Romans i. 17); similarly in Galatians iii. 11–13—" But that no man is justified by the law in the sight of God, it is evident: for the just shall live by faith. . . . Christ hath delivered us from the curse of the law." Luther interpreted these statements in this way: it is true that no works of ours,

[1] *Commentarius in epistolam ad Romanos*, ed. J. Ficker, 1908.
[2] *In epistolam Pauli ad Galatos commentarius*, 1519, Vol. II.

no virtuous feeling or impulse, can assure us of our salvation; these belong to the earthly justice, from which Christ delivered us; but our faith itself is our salvation. " Every Christian should withhold himself from ever wondering if his works are well-pleasing in God's sight; that wonder is his undoing. But if he acts in faith, then the works are necessarily well-pleasing." [1] The criterion of righteousness is to be found in the spirit in which we live, in our faith; if we live in faith, we are saved and aware of our salvation. Personal experience alone gives us the consciousness of salvation, and Luther himself, on discovering this interpretation, suddenly felt a joyful, indubitable consciousness of his own salvation, to which he often referred and of which he was unshake-ably confident. He claimed, indeed, that he had his doctrine " not from men, but from Heaven alone through the medium of our Lord Jesus Christ."

In the final form of his theology, then, Luther identified the certainty of salvation with faith. Both were sheer gifts of God, unconnected with any mental faculties. Thus, while in the first stage of his thought he humbled man to the most despairing helplessness, he now exalted the individual far higher than former theologians had done, making him free of outward observance and intellectual discipline. For the medieval theologians, on the other hand, divine grace had been as it were a philosophical fact which fitted into an intellectual system in a certain relationship with other spiritual facts. Its

[1] *Sermon de triplici justicia*, 1518, Vol. II.

existence in the individual depended on the existence of the rest of this structure. This structure had a twofold nature: it embraced an intellectual, rational system, to which any particular spiritual phenomenon was subordinate; and a social system, the community of believers, on which the individual depended. This was its deepest sense—to bind the individual, intellectually and corporally, in the community; a rationalistic idealism, such as St. Thomas forged, is the strongest and most irrefutable dictatorship. By Luther's time this organisation had broken down, the political system was re-forming itself; and his theological doctrine is the most profound expression of this. By asserting that grace was an irrational quality, which could not be reduced to intellectual terms and whose presence could be detected by the recipient alone, he broke down the medieval relationship between the individual and the Church. But at the same time his doctrine of the evilness of man's will bound the individual irrevocably within the existing social order. No deeds of man could, according to him, be called good in themselves. No social institutions were good in themselves. Goodness consisted only in fulfilling the commands of God, and, as far as the secular order was concerned, these commands could be summed up into: " Render up to Cæsar the things that are of Cæsar." That is, the secular order became for Luther, not the expression of God's wisdom and reason, but of God's power. It was itself of no real value, but a " muck-heap." There was no criterion whereby we could remedy its defects, for our reason is evil and corrupt. The Catholic Church, represented by St. Thomas, had accepted at the base of the secular order certain principles of a divine origin innate in man, such as the idea of justice; this had permitted a revision of secular acts and judgments, in the individual and the State, through a principle higher than the existing powers; it had meant, too, that the secular order was permeated by the Church as the representative of conscience. Luther isolated the two realms, the secular and the spiritual, and while he made the latter subject to the individual conscience, he proclaimed that the former was not within the sphere of human judgment, was sacrosanct.

This doctrine of justification by faith is the central point of Luther's theology. It is completed by the work entitled *On the Freedom of a Christian*,[1] written in the heat of his struggle with Rome, in which he discusses the relationship of the individual to the community. This relationship had been defined by the Church, in the complex subtleties of canon law, in the system of ecclesiastical exercises. By making faith an individual matter, it was necessary for Luther to establish a new basis for the community. In this work he starts from the antithesis: " A Christian is a free man over all things and subject to no man " —" a Christian is a servant to all things and subject to all men "; or, as in 1 Cor. ix. 19: " Though I be free from all men, yet have I made myself servant

[1] Von der Freiheit eines Christenmenschen, Vol. 7.

unto all." The first half of the antithesis, Luther explains, applies to our spiritual part, the soul, the last half to our social part, the body. By faith, through the medium of our soul, we are raised above all things; in the light of faith all commands and injunctions of Holy Scripture and of conscience become merely the expression of our deepest desire; the soul, identified through love with Christ, has complete power over heaven and earth, and is conscious of no restrictions; the believing soul is king and priest. But the Christian is a slave as far as the body is concerned. He mortifies the body, his evil thoughts and desires, for the sake of his cherished faith. His duties to his neighbour are similarly conceived. The believer devotes himself of his own free will to the community in which he is placed; he is a willing slave to his fellow-men. The Christian in his relationship to the world seeks nothing for himself, but desires only to give freely what is his. It is of the greatest importance that he does not do this in order to gain righteousness; the good works he does have no value in God's sight. He acts so simply by the impulse of his faith. Luther uses the analogy: a man who carries out the tasks of a bishop does not thereby become a bishop; rather the bishop accomplishes his proper tasks as the necessary expression of his office.

Thus Luther, after having in the first stage of his thought distinguished faith from reason and the law, now completes his system by defining the relationship of the spiritual and secular worlds. The former alone has divine merit. In the latter neither the ideas of the reason nor social institutions partake in any degree of the divine. Society exists as a means for mortification. It is imposed on us by God as a punishment. It is the representation of God's power, not of His wisdom or goodness. Our duty in the social sphere is to humble ourselves before the law and accomplish the tasks set us, not because they are good, but because they belong to our position. Thus, while on the one hand Luther delivers the soul from the law, making salvation an individual transaction between God and the believer, on the other he delivers over the Christian to the most absolute slavery to the secular law. He allows no possibility of revising this law. In St. Thomas' system there was the possibility of modifying the law by reference to rational ideas, which were of a divine nature; but in Luther's there is no criterion by which the law can be judged; it is merely the will of God. The divine is completely cut off from the worldly; the secular order is made intact.

This liberation of the soul from the bands of the law and delivery of the body to the dominance of the law which Luther proclaimed was a process traceable throughout the Middle Ages. Wiclif and Huss were his most prominent predecessors. And, as Troeltsch points out, the division between natural and divine law, secular and religious affairs, which later medieval theologians insist upon, is an effect of the growing independence of the secular powers, of the development of city-culture. Humanistic thought, too, was an attempt to grapple with the new facts of society. Here, too, the individual was freed, but on one condition—that he subjected himself to the control of reason. Dogma and tradition could be overthrown, but any revolution was to be justified by reason, and a system erected in their place. Thus the rationalism of the humanists left no place in thought for dogma; and in society they would have done away with the Church and priesthood, though they found it expedient to suffer their temporary existence, because of the ignorance and passions of the people. Their thought was entirely secular; and this was their strength and weakness. Because of it, parts of their thought reach right to our times, determining the principles of the individual's attitude towards knowledge; but it had not a wide enough scope. Their rationalism could not prove the existence or non-existence of God, could not analyse revelation and the religious process. As a consequence, they found themselves forced to accept an ultimately divine world-order, even to accept the divinity of Christ. And because they had no interest for these " supernatural " facts, because their thought accepted them without being able to mould them into its system, they could not satisfy the great mass of humanity for whom these were burning questions, who demanded before everything else the assurance of divine solicitude, the assurance of salvation. Luther, on the other hand, made these questions central, and gave a direct answer. Though defying authority up to a point and declaring for a rationalism based on the acceptance of the Bible, and though laying the foundation of a secular ethic, he justified the spiritual side of man by giving it a peculiar law. He could not, any more than the humanists, define the connection between the spiritual and the secular; but, while they slurred over this connection, he stressed this twofold nature of man.

It is natural that the humanists produced no mighty social ethic. While their tendencies were anti-clerical, they lived as a class dependent on privilege, often on the Church, by holding benefices or by profiting by ecclesiastical patronage. They were conscious of themselves as a small, favoured community whose way of life and whose thought could not be applied to the masses without calamity. They were tainted with the anarchical theories which always spring up in an intelligentsia not actively engaged in producing or governing. With Luther it was different: he always felt himself as representative of a community, as leader of his flock. All his doctrine could be immediately translated into action—it was, indeed, accompanied by criticism of facts and incitement to actual reform. He was ready to allow room for an irrational element in his thought without feeling the necessity of bridging over the gap between the irrational and the rational, because both elements supported the same line of action in the social reform, If their form was irreconcilable, their practical realisation was identical. That is to say, by isolating the religious experience in the individual,

Luther took away the *raison d'être* of the Church, and so made the breakdown of the Church possible.

It is to be remarked that the humanists, while welcoming Luther's attempt at bringing the Church back to the simplicity of early Christianity, recoiled before the anarchy which, it seemed, would arise from the application of his doctrine of the absoluteness of the individual conscience. From the trembling poise of their cultured anarchy they feared the rule of the plebs.[1] And, indeed, Luther's early success at defying the papacy gave occasion for many sects of quietists and religious communists to rise, whose doctrines shook the foundations of the social order. A stricter logician than Luther might have been at a loss. He, however, by shifts and modifications showed that his teaching was not to be understood simply, but was a revolutionary expedient. What was valuable in it, besides its tactical use, was the preservation of the irrational element, for this allowed Luther to claim a special, supernatural quality for his dicta. It allowed him to reject the conclusions, the revelations of others, as being " not of God." Without the irrational element he would not have been able to construct any stable belief, any dogma, any church, and the new society would have been at loggerheads with the common ethical system—an unimaginable idea. Luther could thus disregard the fears of the humanists because his thought always contained, perhaps in spite of

[1] See for this and the following remarks *The Formation of the Lutheran Church* (Chap. IV).

appearances, the seeds of a dogmatism, of an organisation, which their rationalism did not.

The evolution of Luther's doctrine of grace has been generally considered as a purely theological development, even by Catholic theologians, who posit the influence of the devil where Protestants see the influence of God. It is true that Luther did not see in 1517 all the implications of this doctrine. Slowly and, it seems, reluctantly, he deduced the theories which are characteristic of the Protestant Church—the rejection of all sacraments but those of baptism and communion, the conception of the Church as the community of all believers, and not merely of the clergy, the repudiation of the papacy, the doctrine of consubstantiation, etc. It is claimed for him, and he claimed for himself, that he wished and hoped for a change of mind within the priesthood, not the disruption of the papacy. But his theological doctrine arose in conscious opposition to the idea of the efficacy of ecclesiastical exercises and penances. He plainly took away from the Church its authority, and gave it to the individual. He struck at the very concept of the Church-State. It is true that he did not realise that the institution of the Church would not voluntarily dissolve itself; nor did he foresee what would take its place. But the meaning of his doctrine was that the Church as an independent secular institution had to be destroyed; this is inextricably interwoven with his religious faith. By what steps he proceeded to the consciousness that the Church must be dissolved is now to be examined.

CHAPTER III

LUTHER'S CONFLICT WITH THE PAPACY

By virtue of his office Luther was able to discuss his doctrine with many of the responsible clergy in Saxony, and won in most places a favourable hearing. His following was strongest in Wittenberg, where he taught and preached—Spalatin at the Court agreed with his new theology, and Carlstadt, formerly a professor in the Thomist theology, began to teach the new doctrine. Staupitz, too, was won over. And all who came in contact with Luther were convinced of his sincerity, and agreed with him on the need for a purification of the priesthood. They began to study St. Paul and St. Augustine, and turned away from the text-books of scholasticism. Luther was never sparing in his criticism of the morals and customs of the clergy, but his chief complaint was that they withheld from their flocks the true word of Christ, the means of salvation. In his sermons of this time (1512–1517) he censured the exaggerated belief in wonders and miracles, in pilgrimages and penances, and combated the priests who encouraged such beliefs; but he did not yet doubt the efficacy of such observances nor the truth of reputed wonders, he still accepted what the Church had canonised. The authority of the Church and the ecumenical councils, even of the Pope, was still unimpeachable for him. His reform was aimed not at the periphery of the papacy, but at its very centre.

Events were bound to reveal the revolutionary nature of his doctrine. In 1517 Luther was brought up against the crassest manifestation of the belief in the power of mere ecclesiastical observance to remit sins—the indulgence—and he was ready to declare himself. The papal indulgence had been originally a method of recruiting for the Crusades against the Turk. It freed the Crusaders from ecclesiastical penances, and consequently from purgatorial pains, and was the counterpart of the Mahommedan belief that those who die for their faith receive the highest heavenly reward. By the twelfth century those who supported the Crusades with gifts of money were promised the same benefits, and from that time it became more commonly used by the Popes as a means of raising money, and came to be recognised as a substitute for penance. The priests to whom the sale of letters of indulgence was entrusted were later given most extensive powers of absolution, so that buyers of indulgences were absolved both from penance and from guilt. The final development of the indulgence was reached at the end of the fifteenth century, when it was claimed that the powers of the indulgence extended to souls already passed to purgatory. The theological justification of the

43

indulgence, which was incorporated into canon law in 1343, was that the Church, as heir of Christ, possessed a treasury of good works—the merits of Christ and the saints—which it could distribute amongst its members, by means of the indulgence; though canon law, as distinct from papalists, never recognised the virtue of the indulgence for souls in purgatory. The development and extension of the powers of the indulgence gives an interesting side-light on the disruptive forces within the unity of the Middle Ages; it shows not only the narrowing of the papacy to a particularist, financial power, but also the break in society between the moneyed, privileged classes and their servants.

In 1515 Pope Leo X issued an indulgence for the archbishoprics of Mainz and Magdeburg and all the Brandenburg territories, nominally for the build-ing of the new St. Peter's in Rome. Albrecht, Archbishop of Mainz and Magdeburg, administered the indulgence. He accepted this rather thankless task—for it was bound to meet with nationalistic opposition [1]—because of his financial difficulties; in order to purchase his pallium he had been forced to borrow on a large scale from the Pope and the Fugger, and this indulgence had been his pledge; as a consequence, agents of the Fugger accompanied the indulgence-preachers, received and checked the moneys collected, and later received half of the

[1] For instance, Duke George of Saxony (not electoral Saxony) refused to allow the indulgence-preachers to enter his lands, on the plea that he had promised this to the Emperor.

proceeds.[1] Albrecht entrusted the sale of the indulgence in electoral Saxony to a lay priest, Tetzel, a man blessed with forcible eloquence, who could well describe the torments of sin, in particular those of souls in purgatory. The indulgence of 1516 was a plenary indulgence. It promised to the buyer, or the person in whose name it was made out, complete remission of the penance for all sins, the promise of divine grace, and deliverance from purgatory; the right to confess to any priest, so that the sinner could choose a lenient priest from whom absolution was certain, and was freed from the control of his parish priest; participation in the general merits of the Church; and, to souls in purgatory, remission of the sins they had committed during their life-time. Except where the promise of divine grace was mentioned there was no word of the necessity of inward repentance.

With the arrival of the indulgence-monger imminent, Luther preached a sermon on the indulgence. He admitted that the Pope, as representative of the Church and Christ, had the power of saving souls in purgatory; also that the indulgence contained the merits of Christ and the saints. A little misgiving forced him to put the question: Can the indulgence really save souls before they truly repent? and if a soul in purgatory has a true will to repent, is it not already saved? He adds, however, " I

---

[1] For more detailed information concerning the conditions of issue of this indulgence see H. Boehmer, *Luther* (London, 1930), pp. 98–101.

confess my ignorance." Soon afterwards Tetzel approached.

Contemporary illustrations show us that the arrival of indulgence-preachers was the sign for a general holiday. They were met with processions and bell-ringing. People flocked in from the surrounding district. Tetzel's case was no exception. He stationed himself at Jüterbog, a town near Wittenberg, and in popular sermons praised the good value of his wares. Luther found his own parishioners flocking to Jüterbog, taking their gulden in their hands. This drain of money from the parish was serious enough; the common purse would suffer appreciably by it. But worse attended on the return of the absolved sinners. For now they were empowered to choose their own confessor, to refuse to go to their parish priest; and when the latter threatened them with punishment, they flaunted the indulgence in his face. Thus the local church was doubly hit; its finances suffered with its prestige. Luther, conscious of his responsibility, protested. His protest took the shape of a challenge to a disputation on the nature and powers of the indulgence; and, as custom would have it, he nailed up on the church door at Wittenberg theses to the number of ninety-five to form a basis for discussion. At the same time he sent notice of his intention to the Archbishop of Magdeburg, Tetzel's master, and to the Bishop of Brandenburg, in whose diocese Wittenberg fell. None of his friends was informed of his action.

The ninety-five theses, nailed up on the church door on October 31st, 1517, do not present a cogent argument, but are a series of points for disputation.[1] A fairly clear line of argument can, however, be detected in them. Luther does not doubt the justification for the indulgence—"Whosoever speaks against the truth of the indulgence shall be anathema and accursed" (71)—but with this formal acquiescence he combines an attack on the accepted idea of the indulgence. He distinguishes between the remission of sin and the penance the Church imposes. The latter is merely the sign of the former (38). And the Pope can remit only the penances which canon law has imposed (5); his indulgence "cannot take away the most insignificant venial sin, in so far as the guilt of this sin is concerned" (76). Luther goes further: "Every Christian who truly repents and sorrows for his sins has complete forgiveness from the penance and guilt, without the indulgence" (36); "every Christian, the living and the dead, participates through God's free gift in the merits of Christ and the Church, without the indulgence" (37); "the true treasure of the Church is the gospel of the glory and grace of Christ" (62). And these statements are supported by the conclusion: "It is a lie and deception to believe that a man shall gain blessedness through the indulgence" (52). Such is the general theme of the theses. Interspersed are other remarks of a more particular nature. "The treasures of the

[1] *Disputatio pro declaratione virtutis indulgentiarum*, Vol. I.

indulgence are in these times the nets in which the riches of men are caught " (66) ; " Christians should be taught that he who gives to the poor and needy does a better deed than if he buys the indulgence " (43) ; and in several theses Luther distinguishes between the real indulgence and the papal intention, on the one hand, and " the licentious and irresponsible words " of the indulgence-mongers on the other, who " preach instead of the commands of the Pope their own phantasies " (70). Towards the end Luther complains of the difficulties which the " acute and cunning questions of the common man " cause the theologian—as, for instance, when it is asked, " If the Pope can, for the mere sake of the building of St. Peter's, deliver so many souls from purgatory, why does he not deliver all souls therefrom out of Christian love? "; and " Why does not the Pope build with his own money instead of with the money of the poor, since he is as rich as Crassus " (82 and 86).

There are three main points in these theses. First, Luther's conception of penance. Together with Staupitz, he had come to the conclusion, based on a study of original documents, that the word " *penitentia* " did not mean an outward exercise, but an inward transformation and repentance. Thus penance was a matter between the individual and God, and the Pope had no power to remit it. Secondly, his conception of the Church. He posited that the Church was not merely the clergy, an earthly and visible institution, but the whole community of believers, a spiritual entity to which all believers belonged. Thirdly, his discernment of the financial basis of the Roman Church. The harmony in his theological and social reform is thus established.

There was a widespread satisfaction that the question of the indulgence was so vigorously broached, and Luther found sympathy in many quarters. The Archbishop of Magdeburg put the matter in the hands of his theologians at Mainz, and gave notice of the doctrines of the monk Luther to the Curia; but he was negligent in business, both theological and ecclesiastic, and did not pursue the matter with energy. His theologians, too, could find nothing legally erroneous in the statements of Luther. The person who was most active was Tetzel, for he was hit in his person and his business. He hurriedly took a doctorate at Frankfort on the Oder, where he found a faculty well disposed towards his cause, and proceeded to counter Luther's theses with some of his own. He contended that Christ had meant, by penance, the ecclesiastical punishments as well as repentance; that the authority of the Pope stood above the decisions of the councils of the Church; that the Pope alone could decide in matters of faith and doctrine and on the meaning of Holy Scripture, and that the Pope was infallible. The papalism which these theses revealed had long been ripening, particularly in Italy, and was supported by a strong body of ecclesiastics; it had furthermore the support of the Order of the Domini-

49

cans, traditional rivals of Luther's Order. We need not consider the fate of these theses of Tetzel's, as his view was contested by more capable champions; it is, however, significant that the immediate answer to Luther's doctrine moved the point at issue to the question of the infallibility of the Pope, and showed the true bearing of his thought to be an attack on the papacy. Tetzel himself died soon afterwards in shame and misery.

The Luther affair was soon taken up by the Curia, and before March 1518 was out, a recantation of his doctrines was demanded of him. He refused. Notice was given that the doctrines would be discussed at the next chapter meeting of the Augustine Congregation to be held at Heidelberg. But already the Elector of Saxony was taking the monk's part, and he refused to let Luther go without an assurance that he would not be harmed. An accusation of Luther was read out at the meeting, but all that was asked of him was that he should send a justification to Rome. There was also a discussion on grace, at which Luther put his interpretation. He won friends at Heidelberg, notably Martin Bucer, then a young monk; and the Congregation was so well disposed towards him that his friend Johann Lang was elected in his place as District Vicar, Luther's term of office having run out. In May Luther sent his Resolutions on the ninety-five theses to Rome, still maintaining his attitude.[1] In a ser-

---

[1] *Resolutiones disputationum de indulgentiarum virtute*, 1518, Vol. I.

with those of the Church, and his declaration that the efficacy of the sacraments was determined by the faith of the participant. The latter point touched Luther's central doctrine of faith, and here he declared he could not recant. They argued together, but came no nearer an agreement. Cajetan himself laid the greatest stress on the former point, in support of which he quoted a bull of Sixtus IV. Luther answered that the bull distorted the meaning of Holy Scripture, at which the legate was aghast; he stated that one had simply to subject oneself to a papal ruling, not to discuss it. The argument came to no end. The next day Luther appeared with an escort of imperial councillors, with Staupitz, and with a notary, before Cajetan, and read out a solemn declaration demanding that before he should be ordered to recant he should be persuaded in a disputation. He begged for permission to lay his case in writing before Cajetan and the Pope. This request the legate granted, and Luther wrote his Justification. This writing treats firstly of the meaning of the bull of Sixtus, analysing words in a scholastic fashion, then of Luther's doctrine of grace, with many quotations from the New Testament. Its chief importance is that in it Luther openly states that papal decrees may err, and that not only does an ecumenical council stand above the Pope, but so also does every believer who arms himself with proofs from the Bible. Such a statement was bound to lead to open recrimination from the papal legate; he supported his arguments with threats of excommunication. Luther wrote letters humble in form to Cajetan, promising to withdraw from the dispute concerning the indulgence if the other side were silent, though still refusing to recognise any error on his part. These letters received no answer; and soon after, Luther, urged by the fears of his friends who dreaded some subterfuge of the papists, slipped out of the town at night and in disguise, and returned home. Within a month of his arriving in Wittenberg, he published an Appellation to a General Council,[1] thus announcing that he no longer had faith in the Pope; and at the same time he wrote to Link, an Augustine monk who had been in Augsburg with him, that he had a shrewd suspicion that the Antichrist of whom Paul speaks ruled at the Roman Court.

During the whole time of his polemic Luther continued to take an active part in parochial work, preaching and teaching the Gospel. Back in Wittenberg he worked at his *Commentary on the Psalms*, one of the most beautiful of his works. Such religious teaching shows him at his best. He reveals in it a depth of feeling and sympathy with spiritual troubles which is rare and which made the people willingly trust him. He has a remarkable gift of translating religious experience through the expressions of the most intimate human relationships, penetrating into the deepest emotive life of his flock. The Curia was meanwhile active. It seems that Cajetan could find nothing definitely heretical in Luther's doctrine

[1] *Appellatio F. Martini Luther ad Concilium*, 1518, Vol. II.

concerning the indulgence, and so he persuaded Leo to issue a bull defining the papal interpretation, and threatening all teaching divergent views with the ban. Immediately afterwards Luther was again summoned to Rome, but again Frederick refused to let him go. The Pope then sent Karl von Miltitz, a noble young German who was Titular Gentleman of the Papal Chamber, to the Elector in order to win him over. Miltitz found great obstacles, and fell back on mediation between Luther's and the papal doctrine. In this he seemed at first to make some progress, but it was strictly beyond his powers. The changed political situation had forced the Pope to adopt slightly different tactics.

In January 1519 Maximilian died, and the rivalry between Francis of France and Charles of Spain for the vacant throne became intense. Both candidates were extremely unwelcome to the Pope, for both were strong princes. He endeavoured to persuade the Elector of Saxony to compete for the throne of the Empire, and did all in his power to win him to this scheme. This was the reason of his renewed affability. But it was without success; and in June Charles was elected Emperor. The Pope, accepting the new situation, once more changed his attitude, recalled Miltitz, and urged on the suit against Luther. The change was signalled by a challenge to a disputation on the points raised at Augsburg, issued against Luther by Eck, a doctor with a reputation for learning who had formerly been an esteemed friend of his.

The disputation took place at Leipzig. Eck defined two main themes: that of grace and that of papal authority. It is significant of the development of the Reformation that Luther deputed his ally Carlstadt to maintain his doctrine on grace, while he reserved to himself the more important task, the attack on the papacy. For four days Carlstadt disputed with Eck. But while Carlstadt was not a great scholar, and in particular had a poor memory, Eck was renowned for his capacious memory and the ease with which he could quote authorities. The disputation was continually held up by Carlstadt's hesitations; he had to beg for time to look up his authorities. Eck, with a huge voice and a butcher-like appearance, overwhelmed his opponent. We need not examine the arguments, as in the end the point at issue was the acceptance or non-acceptance of certain authorities. Then it came to Luther's turn. Here Eck correctly conceived his task, which was to reveal the revolutionary, anarchical consequences of Luther's attitude. Luther's defence of his insubordination towards the Pope was that, in the early history of the Church, the Greek Church and the Greek Fathers were not subordinate to the Pope, and yet their authority was recognised. He referred to the Council of Nicæa (in this argument the historical criticism of humanism came to his aid). There were many expressions of the Fathers of the Church which were antagonistic to papal decrees; did that make the Fathers heretics? Eck pressed him and made him define his attitude to Huss, who had held doctrines similar to Luther's and had been condemned by the Council of Constance. Luther, taken unawares, said that some of the doctrines of Huss were not heretical, even among those which had been condemned. Eck triumphed, for he had brought Luther to the statement that the Ecumenical Council could err. Luther tried to justify himself by saying that in matters of faith a council cannot err, but in other matters it can—a vague and sophistical distinction. At the same time, he showed himself horrified by the thought of a split within the Church.

The outcome of the disputation was then to have clearly pointed to the practical basis and consequences of Luther's teachings. This did not make him more timid, but rather more truculent. The manner in which the disputation was conducted made many of the supporters of Luther's theological and moral reform unhappy. Invectives were hurled at one another by the protagonists, both were constantly in great wrath. From this time on Luther's polemic was carried on in a style which continually called forth rebukes from his friends. His temper was never in control, and he wrote with a hasty, imaginative, savage passion which often led him beyond the bounds of truth and expediency. This passionateness is a reflection of the pressing social issues bound up with his reform; but it was repugnant even to whole-hearted supporters as the gentle Melanchthon and the courtly Spalatin, who were not so directly concerned with the issues; and it repelled the majority of the humanists, whose favourite attitude, that of bland satire, reflected their independence of mass interests and movements.

Soon after the disputation Luther published a pamphlet in which he justified his new standpoint, already called heretical by Eck. In it he insisted on the supreme authority of Holy Scripture and on the right of every individual to interpret belief according to the original documents of Christianity. On this principle he proclaimed that the sacrament of confession was no sacrament, since there was no mention of it in the Bible. This was the first occasion on which he consciously repudiated a recognised dogma of the Church and turned his back on canon law. Still, however, he bridled up on the accusation of frequenting the society of Hussites—that is, sectarians who had broken the unity of the Church. Many of his friends were dismayed at the lengths to which his logic took him, but Melanchthon, a young professor at Wittenberg who brought great learning to his cause, fully approved, and supported him by an examination of the orthodox doctrine of transubstantiation, which he said did not conform to Christ's own statement. Others, too, were struck by the logic of Luther's deductions, and Oecolampadius in Basel and Justus Jonas in Erfurt turned to the study of the Lutheran theology. Luther tried to win over Erasmus to his cause by a flattering letter in which he brought out their common aims, though privately he expressed himself dissatisfied with Erasmus' attitude to grace and salvation. Erasmus never gave a direct answer, being too cautious; he always took the precaution of asserting that he had never read any book of Luther's; at the same time, various statements of his to others show him to have been sympathetic towards Luther at this stage. In the latter part of the year Luther became well acquainted with the writings of Wiclif and Huss, and found much in them that he could whole-heartedly approve, though he distinguished himself from them by saying that his task was primarily to reform theology, whereas theirs had been to reform the Church.

The knowledge of the inevitability of the ecclesiastical ban made this time in Luther's life one of enormous doctrinal development. Nothing now held him back from evolving the consequences of his principles. In the sermon on Repentance [1] he asserted that true contrition would ensure forgiveness of sins; the priest's sanction is not necessary, and the forgiveness may be spoken by any Christian who hears the confession. In the sermon on Baptism [2] he stated that the sacrament of baptism does not ensure our salvation, but takes away only the burden of hereditary acquired sin; it leaves our sinfulness, our concupiscence, still active within us. Similarly, the vows of chastity which monks and priests take, and the sacrament of priesthood, do

[1] *Sermon von dem Sakrament der Busse,* 1519, Vol. II.
[2] *Sermon von dem heiligen hochwürdigen Sakrament der Taufe,* 1519, Vol. II.

not free our nature from sinfulness; that is, the clergy is not a specially favoured order of men, is not spiritually privileged. In the sermon on the Eucharist,[1] in direct connection with the two previous sermons, he repeats that there is no essential difference between the spiritual and secular order, that the Church of Christ is the community of all believers, and that consequently there should be no differentiation in the distribution of the spiritual gifts of the Church; the Eucharist, then, should be administered in both forms, the bread and the wine, to all members of the Christian community. In a letter to Spalatin, Luther wrote: "No sacrament remains for me if there is not an express divine command that it is a means of faith." He was conscious that these attacks on the sacraments of the Church were only part of a general attack on the Church as an institution; historically the sacraments are the means whereby the Church strengthened and renewed its hold on believers. So in the sermon on Good Works [2] he reviewed the harm done to true inward Christian feeling by the forms of the Church, which had led to the belief that faith consisted in the observance of exercises. And in *On the Papacy at Rome* [3] he called Rome the true Babylon and the Pope the Antichrist himself.

But while he was destroying on one side, Luther

---

[1] *Sermon von dem hochwürdigen Sakrament des heiligen wahren Leichnams Christi . . .*, 1519, Vol. II.

[2] *Von den guten Werken*, 1520, Vol. VI.

[3] *Von dem Papsttum zu Rom wider den hochberühmten Romanisten zu Leipzig*, 1520, Vol. VI.

was on the other building up a compensatory system. By the idea that the Church was the community of all believers, both secular and ecclesiastical, he broke down the integrity of the Church; but at the same time he created the possibility of a reform of the Church through the secular powers, he provided the justification for the intervention of the secular powers in the affairs of the Church. So his writings of this and following years refer more and more frequently to the source of strength which Luther could use against the papacy. In February 1519 he wrote to Spalatin: "Only we Germans, to whom the empire came, have strengthened the popes in their power as much as we could. As a punishment we have had to suffer them as masters in cursing and flaying, and now they plunder us by means of pallium-moneys and annates." In the preface to his commentary on the Epistle to the Galatians he praises the German princes for their reluctance to pay papal taxes—"it proves better piety when the princes or whoever it is opposes the Curia, than if they take the field against the Turks." He grows accustomed to using the most violent invective against what were formerly the most sacred of things—"the most accursed Roman Council," etc. It is true that when Ulrich von Hutten, the representative of the dissatisfied, anarchical Estate of imperial knights, wrote to him promising him the armed support of his class, and begging him to move the Elector of Saxony to action, Luther refused to approve his proposals of violence and said the true Gospel must be brought in by the Word, not by force; but Luther was made more confident by these expressions of sympathy, and often in his impulsive way boasted of the armed strength ready for mobilisation behind him. When he heard through the Elector that the Romans were planning to issue the interdict against him, he answered: " Let them take what steps they like, since Schaumburg and Sickingen (two of the most powerful of the imperial knights) have made me secure from the fear of man, a very raging of demons must follow." The armies of the knights, however, ill-organised and irresponsible, would have been his last resort. He hoped very much more from the Elector, from responsible princes, and municipal governments. In the sermon on Good Works (Feb. 1520) he calls on kings, princes, nobles, towns, and parishes, to make a start with the reforms which the Church itself refuses to carry out. In May 1520 he wrote in *On the Papacy at Rome*: " I would be well content if kings, princes, and nobles were to set about razing the streets of the Romish fools. . . . How comes it that the Roman avarice snatches to itself all the places of honour, bishoprics, and fiefs of our cousins?" And he accuses the foreign Italian churchmen of pride and scorn towards the Germans. In resorting to the secular arm to reform the Church, then, Luther revealed clearly how he identified his cause with the national idea, which was already the guiding principle of much of the unrest of the times, and which represented the sum of the interests antagonistic to the Roman Church. He was rallying his forces for the great trial of strength which he knew would soon take place between his cause and the Papacy.

He came to the final formulation of his doctrines in their revolutionary aspect in the three so-called Reformatory writings of 1520.[1] The first, " To the Christian Nobility of the German Nation, concerning the Reform of the Christian Estate," [2] was published in August and was addressed to the Emperor, as the champion of the German nation, as well as to the princes and nobles. Not until 1530, after the Diet of Augsburg held in that year, did Luther give up hope that the Emperor might be won over to his cause against the Papacy; though his prince, Frederick the Wise, understood much earlier that the Emperor was as much an enemy as the Pope. As the title of this work indicates, it is an appeal to the secular authorities themselves to take in hand the reform of the Church. Luther begins by counselling moderation and caution in dealing with the weighty affairs of the Church. Then he develops his theme. The Romanists have built round them three walls to protect themselves from being reformed. The first wall is the doctrine of the secular power of the Church. This Luther says is not justifiable, and contrary to Holy Scripture.

[1] It must be noted that it was the revolutionary aspect which was chiefly stressed in these writings: other aspects, though implicit, were not developed till later. See Chaps. IV and V.
[2] *An den christlichen Adel deutscher Nation von des christlichen Standes Besserung*, 1520, Vol. VI.

He adduces the revelation of the Italian humanist Valla concerning the falsity of the legend of the gift of temporal power to the Church by the Emperor Constantine—this work of Valla's had been published in Germany shortly before by Hutten. The Church, Luther re-asserted, is the community of all Christians, and it is impossible to divide churchmen from laymen, just as it is wrong to give the Church an earthly body. The secular powers have been appointed by God to protect the Christian community and to control secular affairs, the princes of the Church exist to look after the spiritual welfare of Christians and to preach God's word. Each estate, the lay and the ecclesiastical, has the duty of correcting the other if that other inadequately fulfils its task. Luther refutes the claim of priests to be immune from secular law, and attacks the idea of clerical courts of law. The second wall the papists have erected is their assertion that the Pope's interpretation of the Bible and his decision in matters of faith are definitive; Luther quotes many passages from the New Testament to refute this, and claims for every believer the right of interpreting the Bible. The third wall is the papists' claim that only the Pope may call a council of the Church, which Luther refutes similarly by reference to the first documents of Christianity and on the basis of his new definition of the Christian Church.

Luther then goes on to a more detailed criticism of ecclesiastical abuses. In twenty-five paragraphs he scourges the pride and avarice of the Pope; the simony and pluralism rife amongst the princes of the Church; the lavishness of the papal court, with its burden of unoccupied officials all waiting for fat benefices to fall vacant. He attacks the extortionate annates, the favouritism in the bestowal of benefices, the trade in the gift of pallia. He complains of the usury at Rome. Such complaints were the stock-in-trade of every reformer and satirist of the time; they were brought up by the imperial Estates at the Diet of Augsburg in 1518, by hosts of writers, by responsible clergy such as the Bishops of Chiemsee and Liège. But Luther's proposal of reform differed from that of other ecclesiastics. He puts the responsibility of reform in the hands of the secular powers. Every prince, noble, municipality, should forbid its subjects to send annates to Rome; the Christian lords should oppose the bestowal of benefices to aliens. Luther proposes that the national bishops should form a council of government for their country and ratify new bishops without reference to the Pope; the national Church should in most things be independent of the Pope, whose function should be that of theological arbiter.

Luther then goes over to more particular questions. He attacks the institution of begging monks, so useless and pernicious a body, and proposes that they should be regularised. Monasteries, he says, should be under the control of the bishops, and should become what they originally were intended to be—schools. He would give leave to monks to quit their monasteries if they so wished, and condemns the vow of celibacy, which he calls a human device to send men to the devil. He then attacks several of the ordinances of the Church, such as fasting and dispensations from penances, and says they were instituted merely to produce money. There are too many ceremonies, too many holy days, too many rites, so that the common man is confused, and encouraged to superstition; and all for the sake of increasing the Church's income. Luther gives advice incidentally as to the care of the poor, making each parish responsible for its own poor. He proposes another investigation of the Hussite heresy. Turning to the sacrament of communion, he says the cup should be given to lay as to spiritual members of the Church; and he calls the Catholic doctrine of transubstantiation erroneous, accepting Melanchthon's teaching of consubstantiation, which replaced the Aristotelian Thomist antithesis of accident and substance with the less rationalistic idea that Christ was in the bread and wine as the soul is in the body.

Luther discusses secular matters. In the universities there is not enough pure Gospel taught, and too much logic, physics, ethics, metaphysics, according to the pagan Aristotle, who denies the immortality of the soul and the grace of God. Luther would permit the study of Aristotle's Logic, Rhetoric, and Poetic, providing they were studied without the medieval scholastic commentaries; and the rest he would replace by Latin, Greek, Hebrew, mathematics, and history. Canon law should be torn out by the roots—the Popes themselves have no respect for their own law, and continually substitute their own judgments for the legal ones. Theological books must be combed out, for they prevent us from studying the true source of Christianity. Schools must be endowed where girls as well as boys may study and hear the Gospel. Luther closes with a short list of the sins common among the secular Estates—their arrogance and pride, the extravagance of their customs and clothing, their use of foreign luxuries, spices and silks, the gluttony, drunkenness, and debauchery which are general; and he attacks a practice which was becoming widespread, the levying of interest on money-loans—" but the greatest misfortune of the German nation is without doubt the taking of interest," which has thrown so many princes and cities into poverty; there must be control of the money-dealers, one must " put a bridle on the Fugger and such-like societies "; it would be best for Christians to leave trade and take to agriculture again. Finally, he prays that the Christian nobility of the German nation will have the spiritual courage to do its best for the poor Church.

This work of Luther's covers an astonishing range. In it he for the first time recognises the conditions and consequences of his theological doctrine: he reveals himself fully as social reformer. He advocates not merely a change of heart, but a change of constitution. The Church shall be no longer the controller of the secular arm; above all, the Church shall not be controlled from Rome. It must be noticed that Luther does not envisage the dissolution of the Church as an organisation. He does not attack the idea of a priesthood, but merely defines the scope of the Church. There is an anomaly in his doctrine that the bishops should have certain powers which he refuses to the chief representative of the Church, the Pope. Here the chief characteristic of this work comes to light: Luther calls for action on national grounds. Much more than the antithesis secular-ecclesiastical the antithesis national-papal is the force behind his agitation; the nationalistic idea is predominant. The word " German " appears repeatedly, and Luther's case on the national issue is so strong that he can appeal to German ecclesiastical as well as secular lords to carry through his proposed reforms and cast off the Roman yoke. National action on the part of the German bishops might well have been envisaged; [1] but there was so great a lack of political unity in Germany, however, that it was impossible, for a national cause could not solve particularist antagonisms. And by his doctrine of the right of intervention in ecclesiastical affairs on the part of the temporal powers, Luther had made co-operation between ecclesiastical and temporal lords more difficult, for the former would be subjected to the latter if they broke away from Rome—except of course in the case of ecclesiastical

[1] Cf. the attempts of Berthold of Mainz, an ecclesiastical prince, to unify Germany at the beginning of the sixteenth century. [Ranke, *Geschichte im Zeitalter der Reformation*, Vols. I and II.]

lords who were at the same time independent secular princes. The work was to find all the more sympathy amongst the German princes, who could look on it as a manifesto of their own claims, as it was to some extent of every secular party in the Empire.

In September 1520 the papal ban against Luther was published. It contained a description and condemnation of his errors and gave him sixty days in which to decide to recant. It demanded that all his works containing any of these errors should be burned. Luther's answer was the second of the great reformatory works—*On the Babylonian Captivity of the Church.*[1] He had had this work in his mind for some time as a flea for the ear of the Pope, and its criticism is more disruptive than that of the preceding writing. He attacks in it the very foundation of the Church, the sacraments on which it had consolidated its domination. He sanctions only those sacraments which are expressly enjoined by Holy Scripture, and his arguments are based entirely on the authority of the New Testament. He disproves the legitimacy of all the sacraments except three—baptism, communion, and confession; later, of course, he was to reject the last as well. The sacraments of confirmation, of priesthood, of extreme unction, and marriage he says are no true sacraments. Concerning marriage, he says it confers no special blessing or privilege on the parties, but he is, with the Church, opposed to divorce. He would rather have bigamy than divorce, though he would

[1] *De captivitate Babylonica Ecclesiæ præludium,* Vol. VI.

not prevent the guiltless party from marrying again. Here the difference between his and the Church's conception of marriage is visible. For the Catholic Church marriage is a contract with God, no faithlessness of one party can excuse that of the other; for Luther it is a contract between two humans, sacred while both keep faith, but unbinding on the one if the other commits adultery. This is characteristic of Luther's thought, which secularised morals, drawing a sharp dividing line between God's affairs and man's. So also in the Catholic doctrine of transubstantiation, which Luther refutes in this work, the natural and divine were reconciled in the idea that the " substance " of the sacred elements was Christ, and the " accidents " natural. Luther could not accept this systemisation of God, and supported Melanchthon's view that Christ was as distinct from the elements as our soul is from our body. The " Babylonian Captivity " shows the application of Luther's principles rather than their justification.

On the day of the publication of this work, the University of Wittenberg received the papal bull, and debated what action it should take. Some of Luther's friends advocated appeal to the Emperor, so rooted was the idea that the Empire was the natural antagonist to the Church, that the Emperor represented the temporal interests of the Germans. Even Luther expressed his regret that Charles did not correct the papists. It is true that now and again Charles showed signs of wishing to reform certain abuses in the Church, but he never allowed himself to consider the reformation of doctrine; and we shall see how, at Worms in 1521, it was the chief task of the papists not to allow these two issues to be separated, for fear of a violent purification of the condition of the Church. But the Emperor could not further the breakdown of the Papacy. The consequent strengthening of the temporal princes would have led immediately to a weakening of his own power. And Charles followed the policy which seemed most advantageous for him.

Before any steps were taken as a result of the bull, Luther published the third reformatory work—*On the Freedom of a Christian*.[1] To this he attached an open letter to the Pope, Leo, couched in the most humble, even servile, terms, begging the Pope (he calls him " most holy ") to free himself from his evil counsellors and to listen to the voice of truth. He asks for a reconciliation, assuring Leo of his utmost reverence, though stating that he cannot take back anything he has said about the institution of the Papacy. This missive is remarkable in that it shows, as well as an excessive naivety, that Luther was in no way opposed to the idea of priesthood, of a possible orthodoxy, in spite of his principles.[2] In the work itself we see the same underlying principles as in Luther's interpretation of marriage and the Eucharist. While the Catholic Church had attempted to draw soul and body into one

---

[1] *Von der Freiheit eines Christenmenschen*, Vol. VII; see pp. 35 ff.   [2] Cf. Chap. IV.

system—expressed most strikingly by the doctrine of the spiritual efficacy of outward observances—Luther defined them as belonging to two incompatible spheres. No earthly acts have for him any spiritual validity. This was the metaphysical basis on which his attack on the Papacy was founded, and it was to have far-reaching political consequences. At the same time, though Luther dwells on the ineffable joy of the soul's communion with God and finds tender, intimate words to describe it, it is false to accuse him of mysticism or quietism, as some Catholic historians have done. The aim of the Christian is not, according to this conception of Luther's, to lose himself in his faith; his faith expresses itself necessarily in actions, in dogmas. He wishes only to revise the relationship between good works and faith, as it is defined by Catholic theology, not to do away with the necessity of good works. There is, however, a serious logical fault in his attitude which was to have practical results of great importance.[1]

The principles of Luther's reform were now defined. The time for action had come. The arrival of the papal ban made decisions inevitable. In many districts in Germany there was consternation; many bishops would not act without first consulting the secular lords in their diocese, and the reluctance of the secular powers to act can be judged by the fact that in 1518 the Estates had protested in the Diet against the execution of papal

[1] Cf. *Luther and the Sects*, Chap. IV.

74

bulls if unsupported by an imperial decision. The University of Wittenberg discussed openly how it could avoid putting the bull into effect, and it found its excuse in the methods of procedure adopted by Eck, whom the Pope had entrusted with the promulgation of the bull in Germany. Eck did not dare personally to enter electoral Saxony, and the bull was obeyed only half-heartedly in the adjoining bishoprics of Meissen, Merseburg, and Naumburg. The Pope sent a special message to the Elector urging him to carry the bull into effect, but Frederick was wary. He asked advice of Spalatin, who of course stood by his friend, and of Erasmus, who, though not pro-Lutheran, said the monk had not been given a proper hearing and should not be given up till that had occurred; he said, further, that the whole attitude of the papists was due to their hatred of the new learning, of the new method of going back to original texts. Erasmus took sides then purely on the formal issue. In the end Frederick decided to give Luther his protection until he had been given a fair trial under non-partisan judges. Luther himself was asked by the Elector and Spalatin to answer the charges enumerated in the bull; we need not examine his answer, for it recapitulates the old arguments. He also gave more practical advice in his *Against the Bull of the Anti-Christ*,[1] the title of which indicates the spirit in which it was written. He says it seems impossible that the bull is genuine; but, if it is so, then he

[1] *Wider die Bulle des Endchrists*, Vol. VI.

will answer proudly, confident of his right as a Christian to judge in matters of faith. He discusses not the rightness or wrongness of his doctrine, but the right of overthrowing decisions of the Pope, and threatens the Church again with the judgment of the secular powers. Once more he appeals for a general council of the Church, though whether as a bluff or out of confusion of mind one cannot say, for he had already, at Leipzig, said that councils could err, thereby refusing to bind himself to the pronouncements of any council.

With the Emperor, meanwhile, the papal cause was advancing. The Pope had sent Aleander, a former papal librarian and a very clear-sighted politician, to treat with Charles, and considerable success attended his efforts. The Imperial Council, it is true, refused to ratify the project of a law which required the extermination of Luther's doctrines, books, and followers, but Aleander persuaded the Emperor to issue a press ordinance directed against Luther's teachings, and to decree for his hereditary lands the destruction of Lutheran books. And so in certain places, notably in the Netherlands, but also in several strongholds of scholasticism, as Cologne, there were solemn burnings of Luther's books. This action stirred Luther, and, after deliberation with Spalatin, he declared that if a like auto-da-fe occurred at Leipzig, as was just then threatened, he would retaliate by burning at Wittenberg the works of his antagonists. In the general excitement, however, he acted before anything occurred at Leipzig. A public notice was posted up summoning all professors and students to a gate of the town. There, on a bonfire lit by Melanchthon, Luther solemnly committed to the flames the papal bull, the books of canon law, and the papal decretals. It was a symbol of the complete rupture with the Catholic Church, a proclamation that Luther no longer hoped for a reformation from within the Church. On the next day he declared in a lecture: " If you do not with your whole hearts renounce the papal rule, your souls cannot win blessedness! " He justified his act by claiming the right of every Christian to destroy what he thinks to be of danger to his neighbours, and expressed the hope and belief that he acted inspired by the Holy Ghost. He told Staupitz later that he had at first been afraid to come to the decision, but that, having taken it, he was " gladder over this deed, once having dared it, than over any other deed in his whole life." In his instructions to his adherents, as to how they should behave on the matter of the forbidden books when questioned by their confessors, he says, confessors ought not to question their flocks about his books. If they insist, however, and try to worry the books out of the possession of their parishioners, then, says Luther, " quit sacrament, altar, parson, and church," and rely on your own conscience and the Word of God. He adds a word on the confession itself, saying only tradition has made it a sacrament, thus completing his reduction of the sacraments of the Church.

And he found time, amidst all this invective and polemic, to write one of his most generous religious works, his commentary on the Magnificat.[1]

The papists continually pressed Charles to issue the imperial ban against Luther, but he was unable to do so. In his own hereditary realm of Spain there was a strong anti-papal party, which had already protested against the high-handedness of the papal action with regard to Luther; and the general political situation, the enmity of France, and the unreliability of the papacy as a temporal factor, made coercive action risky. The Elector Frederick played skilfully. He opposed all attempts to deal summarily with Luther by two objections: firstly, that Luther was willing to submit to a disputation and would recant his errors if he were persuaded that he was in the wrong; secondly, that, according to a clause of the election capitulation of Charles V, the Emperor could not pronounce the imperial ban without a trial, except by consent of the imperial Estates. Frederick was successful in gaining his aim: that Luther should be given public hearing before the Estates of the Empire, where he would be assured of very great sympathy. He insisted, too, that the imperial citation summoning Luther to trial at the Diet should include a safe-conduct covering the time of his absence from Saxony. And by Frederick's refusal to deliver the citation himself to Luther, the Emperor was forced to send it to the rebellious monk through an imperial herald,

[1] *Das Magnificat verdeutschet und ausgelegt*, 1521, Vol. VII.

much against his will and to the great vexation of the papal party. It was the papists' hope that Luther would not come to the Diet of Worms, so that he could be condemned in contumacy. When they found that he was determined to come, they, working hand in glove with Charles, tried various subterfuges to hold him up. At the last moment an imperial mandate was issued stating that the Emperor and Empire would tolerate no changes of doctrine, and would merely call on Luther to recant; in the case of his refusal, he would be dealt with as the Holy See demanded. This document reached Luther at Frankfurt, when he was on his way to Worms, and it was hoped that, alarmed by the prospect of a summary judgment, he would not continue on his way. Similarly, the Emperor's confessor got into touch with Sickingen, the imperial knight, whose castle was only a few hours' journey from Worms, and tried to side-track Luther there, where he could have been held up long enough to have ensured his absence from the proceedings of the Diet. But Frederick and Luther were too wise for their opponents, and to the great consternation of the papal party, Luther arrived in Worms in a sort of triumphal procession, preceded by the imperial herald and surrounded by his friends, and took up quarters with the retainers of his prince.

The Luther affair was already considerably advanced before Luther arrived at Worms. At first the atmosphere was rather favourable to the Pope's cause, as the letters of the Elector of Saxony show.

Aleander, the papal legate, used bribes and promises cleverly; his despatches to the Pope continually urge the bestowal of gifts and benefices at critical moments and to important men, and he used this method of persuasion with success, winning over the Emperor's confessor, the Elector of Brandenburg, and other less important notabilities. Aleander diagnoses the whole situation in the most practical way. The Elector Frederick, he says,[1] is disaffected because a natural son of his was ignored at Rome; the princes support Luther simply because they covet the property of the Church; they are all indignant that their favourites have been passed over in the bestowal of benefices; like a true Roman diplomatist, Aleander sums up his attitude in these words: "There is no better way of calming these enraged minds than by gifts." So far as he went he was right. The dissatisfaction had economic causes. But he was wrong in supposing that any such palliative as isolated gifts would satisfy the greed of the princes. The Curia itself was even further away from estimating the true scale of dissatisfaction.

After much persuasion, Aleander got the Luther affair discussed in the Diet. He gave a three-hour speech on the heresy. Skilfully he spoke little of that part of Luther's doctrine which dealt with the supremacy of the Papacy and its relationship with the secular power, but dwelt on the rebellious agitation in his work, the incitement to disturb the

---

[1] Paul Kalkoff, *Die Depeschen des Nuntius Aleander vom Wormser Reichstag*, 1521. Halle, 1886.

peace of Empire and Church, comparing him with Huss, whose doctrine had led to civil wars and revolts. But though there was a visible danger of popular revolt in Luther's doctrines, there was too much in them which appealed to the princes for the latter to accept Aleander's analysis. The Electors refused to condemn Luther out of hand, though they almost came to blows in the heat of argument. In the end the citation was sent off to Luther, on the grounds that he had done so much for the common people and had such influence among them that it would imperil the princes' authority to endorse the anathema of the Church without even the semblance of a trial. In effect, the Estates insisted that judgment and execution should be in their hands. And they were so clear as to their interests that they proposed, too, that if Luther recanted his theological errors they should proceed to a discussion of his teachings concerning ecclesiastical abuses and papal authority. This was exactly what Aleander dreaded, for if the two matters were separated, he knew that the princes would readily sacrifice Luther on the theological issue if they could have their own way with ecclesiastical reform. He went so far as to exhort the Pope rapidly to carry through some measure of purification of the Church, even at great cost, in order to disarm the princes. In the end, however, his influence with the Emperor was powerful enough to prevent the two issues from being separated.

Such was the state of things amongst the rulers

when Luther entered Worms. Among the common people, among the burghers, feeling was more simple. At several towns on his route Luther was met by civic receptions. Friends accompanied him on his way, and knights provided an escort. The common people and the lower officials at Worms all felt his cause to be theirs—Aleander, for instance, had constant difficulties with the lower imperial officials, with printers and translators, who refused to do his work without substantial bribes, while pro-Lutheran leaflets and pamphlets often appeared. Soon after his arrival, Luther was cited before the diet.[1] The official from Treves, a secular office-holder who had no powers of disputation, was put in charge of the " trial." He simply set Luther the question: would he retract all his books or not? This was the form most favourable to the Papacy, for it prevented enumeration and analysis of the separate issues. Luther, speaking in a small, timid voice, asked for time to consider, and this was granted. It surprised many that he asked for this postponement, for the form of the trial had been made clear beforehand. The next day the official asked him if he were ready to defend all his books,

---

[1] Luther had come to Worms fresh from a controversy with Hieronymus Emser in which the titles of the pamphlets indicate the temper of the dispute:—Emser—Against the unChristian book of Luther *To the Christian Nobility*; Luther—To the Goat of Leipzig (a play on Emser's coat-of-arms); Emser—To the Bull of Wittenberg; Luther—On the answer of the Leipzig Goat; Emser—On the raging reply of the Wittenberg Bull; Luther—Answer to the superchristian, superclerical, super-cunning book of Goat Emser—Luther surpassed everyone in force of invective.

Title-page of Ulrich von Hutten's Gesprächbüchlein (Dialogues)
1521. Luther and Hutten are associated in the illustration

[*To face p.* 83.

or would retract some. Luther answered this time
in a clear voice. He divided his books up into
three categories: books of edification, commentaries
on devotional themes, with which no one would
quarrel and which he could not withdraw; books
against the Papacy and the papal tyranny—if he
retracted these, he said, he would merely open
wider the door to papal oppression and the reign of
Antichrist; books against particular persons, which
he confessed were sometimes over-violent, but which
he could not retract without strengthening the cause
of false doctrine and tyranny. He begged finally
for a proper trial on the questionable points, for a
disputation. The official answered, he had merely
to answer the questions set him, not to dispute; it
was not a matter for a council. Why, he asked,
did Luther insist on a council, when his doctrines
had already been condemned by councils? Luther
countered by saying that councils had erred, and he
wished for a fresh judgment; if this were not granted,
he would not recant one jot of his teaching. With
this challenge Luther left the Diet, and leaving, he
raised his arm above his head like a German knight
when he has struck a good blow. He had put his
case well, for he had accentuated the tyrannicalness
of the Pope, the common cause of discontent between
him and the Estates, and had shown that he had
not been given a trial. From the Ebernburg,
Sickingen's castle, Hutten sent him fiery letters of
encouragement; and a notice was nailed up everywhere, announcing a league of 400 German knights

against the papists, signed " Bundschuh, Bundschuh, Bundschuh," the sign of the rebels in the bloody peasant revolts of some years before. Any other outcome than this open antagonism of papists and Lutherans was impossible. Luther had come determined to demand a disputation in which he would have refused to recognise any of the authorities the other side adduced; and Aleander had written before his arrival: " I have no hope of converting this obstinate heretic."

Luther's open declaration was exactly what Aleander had worked for. But the Estates were still reluctant to ratify the papal ban. He was summoned before a committee of the Estates. The great stumbling-block in the way of a reconciliation was his statement that an ecumenical council could err, for no churchman, no man who valued the unity of the Church, could tolerate such an attitude. Cochlaeus, a humanistic churchman, visited him several times in a few days, but he could not move Luther, for those doctrines of Luther's which referred to the nature of the Church were amongst those of Huss which had been condemned by the Council of Constance. Luther and Frederick, his prince, being convinced of the hopelessness of further negotiation, asked for the promised safe-conduct, which extended over a period of twenty-one days. After that time Luther would be at the mercy of any lord in whose territory he happened to be. With this safe-conduct he left Worms. He went off serenely in the direction of Wittenberg.

Though he was under an obligation not to preach, he could not restrain himself, and spoke to the people at one or two places on the way, justifying himself with the statement that "God's word cannot be bound." Then, suddenly, he disappeared. A tumult arose at Worms, for it was believed that the papists had carried him off, and Aleander went in fear of his life. The legate, however, fell immediately on the correct explanation—Luther was abducted, after a pretence of hostility, by servants of his own prince, and was taken to the Wartburg, a castle of the Elector's, where he would be safe from the papists and incapable of causing fresh disturbances. There he remained in hiding for a year, working at devotional tasks, at his translation of the Bible, and often fretting over the course of the reform. In the end, dangerous troubles amongst his own flock caused him to return to Wittenberg, against the wish of his lord; but as the Emperor was preoccupied with wars, and there was no danger of an intervention, he was allowed to stay on.

After Luther's departure from Worms obstinate discussions still went on in the Diet. There could be no doubt that the papal ban was just, but the Estates were unwilling to act as the henchmen of the Papacy, and also to lose the advantages Luther's reform movement promised. It was the aim of the princes of the Empire to divide the two issues, allowing the condemnation of Luther on theological grounds, and considering the question of the reform of the Church separately. To this end, the jurists, both secular and ecclesiastical, of the German princes bent their powers, supporting this aspect of Luther's doctrine in spite of the fact that Luther had attacked them and their office most determinedly. Aleander, knowing that if such a policy were successful a violent purging of the Church would ensue, opposed it with all his skill, and Charles, who realised that his own position rested on the same authoritarian system as the Pope's, threw his influence into the balance on the side of Aleander. The Diet dragged on. The princes became anxious to get back to their domestic affairs. War was preparing between France and the Emperor. Many of the members of the Estates went away, including the Electors of Saxony and the Palatinate, leaving in the supreme Estate two temporal and three ecclesiastical electors. Before this depleted assembly the imperial ban was at last pronounced against Luther. It proclaimed that Luther had repeated old heresies and developed new which would lead to revolt, murder, and conflagration in Church and Empire; no one should give him shelter, food, or drink; nor tolerate his books; and it was the duty of all to take him where he was to be found and to hand him over to imperial justice. A general censorship of books was proclaimed. At the same time, the Emperor made a treaty with the Pope against the French, and he left the Diet with a promise of support in his war from the Estates. In such a situation there was no prospect of the ban's being immediately enforced.

The Diet of Worms represents the climax in the antagonism between Luther and the Papacy, the climax of Luther's revolutionary activity. After this time, when the principles of reform are assured, the initiative was taken out of his hands and went to others. Up to this moment all discontented parties were ranged under his lead—the particularist princes, the anarchical knights, the bourgeoisie in the towns, the dispossessed workers, the peasants. Now came the time for these parties to act on the declaration of rights which Luther had made. And while he hung back they severally tried to achieve their ends. All that was left for Luther to do was to show to which party he belonged; his rôle was now, not to incite, but to sanction. As a consequence, the most satisfactory method of study of Luther, from 1521 onwards, is to examine his connexion with the movements and forces set loose by his appearance at Worms. From this point, therefore, a strictly chronological study will be abandoned. But before going over to the various movements which ensued, it is of advantage to pass in review those points in the succeeding years which seemed critical for the whole Reformation, *i.e.* those points at which it seemed possible that the rebels against the Emperor's and Pope's authority might be quelled and the schism in Christendom healed.

Until 1525 no general action against the Lutherans could be contemplated by the Emperor and the supporters of the papal cause, because of the wars with France. There were continual defections to the side of the reformers because of the military misfortune of the Emperor, which meant not only that he was weak, but also that he could not pay clamorous creditors. The obvious profit resulting from the non-payment of ecclesiastical taxes as from the expropriation of ecclesiastical property was a great seduction to secular lords. But in 1525 the imperial troops won a decisive victory over the forces of France at Pavia. The war came to an end. Charles was the recipient of reparation payment, and many banking-houses offered him subsidies; he could conciliate many disaffected subjects by paying off old debts, notably those contracted during his election campaign. And when the Diet met at Augsburg, he found a considerable body of friends. It was there decided to fulfil the ban of 1521 against the Lutherans, but the Diet was adjourned till the following year, in order to consider measures of action and to achieve unanimity. There was, however, by this time an open Lutheran party, led by the Elector of Saxony and the Landgrave of Hesse, which was determinedly opposed to any attempt at rescinding the privileges it had assumed. Partisan feeling was much more bitter because of the persecution of members of both faiths which had taken place in Catholic and Lutheran lands. And so, when the Diet met at Speyer in 1526 to take the final decision, it found a Lutheran union in existence, the League of Torgau, whose members were sworn to mutual aid against any offensive of the papists. But a change in the international situation was even more fatal to Charles' intentions. Clement VII, a scheming but short-sighted Pope, fearful of the unchallenged domination of the Emperor, concluded a league with his former enemy, Francis of France, expressly aimed at Charles. From the south the Turks were advancing against the Empire. Charles, faced by so many enemies, could not afford to raise revolt in Germany. For the sake of military support against his enemies he came to an arrangement with the Lutheran party, whereby all princes were allowed, for the time being, to rule as they wished in their own lands, and to encourage which religion they chose. This decision was of incalculable importance in the history of the schism. Lutheranism became for the first time a recognised, legalised religion, instead of a condemned heresy; even the confiscation of ecclesiastical property was condoned.

In 1528 the Catholic princes of Germany decided, although the Emperor was engaged elsewhere, to launch an attack on their Lutheran enemies. An armed clash seemed inevitable, but again the position of foreign affairs saved Germany. The momentary lull in European antagonisms round 1530 again made preparation for action possible. At the Diet of Augsburg there was a formal examination of the Lutheran tenets, Melanchthon being charged with the statement of the Lutheran point of view. This was, as before, condemned, and the Emperor and papists prepared to take violent measures against his rebellious subjects; the Protestants, on their part, took up a much more belligerent attitude. But again the Turks intervened, and Charles was compelled once more to postpone his plans for the internal settlement of Germany. He made a peace with the Protestants, the "Common Peace" of Nürnberg, 1532, in which he gained the co-operation of the Protestants at the price of recognising their religion. As far as the confiscation of church property was concerned, the status quo was accepted. What was more important was that Protestants and Catholics treated with one another as if they were independent autonomous powers. By this time the Protestant powers had so entrenched themselves that only a bloody war would oust them; the idea of the overlordship of the Emperor was shaken to its foundations. But the story of the growth of independence is not complete till the Religious Peace of Augsburg, 1555, when not only was complete freedom of choice allowed to each prince in religious matters, but also in political matters the right of making alliances with foreign powers. This denoted the complete breakdown of the medieval empire.

The outstanding effect of Luther's attack on the traditionalists, both theological and ecclesiastical, was, then, that his doctrine secured enough support to affirm itself permanently in certain parts of Germany. Some states accepted Lutheranism, and, with it as their banner, affirmed the political independence they had long been working for; they fought for and established a Lutheran Church. But what was the relationship between this result

and the principles Luther in the beginning pro-
pounded? What was this Lutheranism? What this
Lutheran Church? Luther had said that the Church
was the community of all believers; that all men
were spiritual members of the community as they
were also lay members; that what was necessary
was the breakdown of clericalism and the individualisation of religion. Whence came this connexion between the policy of princes and the
renewal of religious life? By the successive pacts
and by the final settlement of 1555 between Catholics
and Protestants, the princes were given the right of
deciding what religion their lands should follow;
but this has nothing to do with the right of self-
determination of the individual in religion, which
was Luther's trump-card in his disputations with
the papists. The existence of two opposing dogmas
was thereby recognised, nothing more. The answer
might be: This political development, these political
pacts, were the skeleton upon which Luther could
build his inward and fundamental reform; he himself accepted them as an expedient which the times
thrust upon him, but worked for an eventual
removal of such anomalies. This answer has often
been given; an historical investigation of the
questions raised will decide whether it is correct
or no.

CHAPTER IV

THE FORMATION OF THE LUTHERAN CHURCH

(a) *Luther and the Sects*

In spite of the turmoil of practical affairs into which
he was thrown after 1517, Luther always considered
himself essentially a theologian. He repeated again
and again that he came to renew theology, to in-
augurate a purely religious reform, and once distinguished himself from Huss by defining the latter
as essentially an ecclesiastical reformer. For Luther
the reform of morals was of a very minor importance.
He considered that manners would reform automatically if the pure religion were adopted. In this
he differed radically from the humanists, for whom
the reform of morals was the essential. He attacked
most bitterly what he constantly referred to as the
epicurean attitude, *i.e.* that attitude which considered
all problems from a merely human view-point without taking into account divine influence. On this
score he reviled Erasmus, and would not believe that
this " sceptic," this " epicurean," died uttering the
pious words: " Jesus, thou Son of God, have pity
on me." He was able to express such an extreme
hatred for the Turks and to call for their extermination for this very reason, warning men against the

hypocritical appearance of morality and religiosity in which Mohammed's doctrine and adherents were clothed. Similarly, he says of the pagan Greeks: " The wisdom of the Greeks, when compared with that of the Jews, is bestial." True faith, true religion, surpassed incomparably all other values. The main points of Luther's theology are: (1) To be a Christian one must have faith, and this in itself atones for all one's sin; to have perfect faith is identical with the sure knowledge of salvation. (2) Salvation and the remission of sins are a personal matter between the believer and God which is not affected by the intercession of others; good works have no effect, neither ecclesiastical rites nor penances. (3) Man cannot therefore work out his salvation; the grace of God is bestowed freely without consideration of his deserts; man has no freedom of will. (4) The foundation of religion is the New Testament, which is open to the interpretation of each individual. Any believer can, on the authority of Holy Scripture, combat the decisions of the Fathers of the Church, the ecumenical councils, and the Popes. Luther's doctrine in its first form was implicitly anti-clerical, and did away with the necessity of the priesthood. Anyone filled with the Holy Ghost was called on to preach the Word of God. Those sacraments which remained—communion and baptism—were to be administered by any member of the congregation. Luther counted on a new spirit infusing the world, so that everyone would carry out the duties his secular position imposed on him with an ever-present

93

consciousness of his spiritual nature. The old ecclesiastical forms would of themselves wither away.

Resting on this belief, Luther did not make dispositions for positive steps of reform. The consciousness of his responsibility to his prince and his flock made him timorous, for it was not easy to reconcile the desires of both. Some of his followers, however, were clearer as to their needs. While Luther was at the Wartburg he heard of disturbances at Wittenberg. Priests were violently prevented from celebrating private Mass, a practice Luther himself had condemned. Uneasy, he went secretly to Wittenberg, where he found things not so bad as he had feared; but he was incensed to find that Spalatin had suppressed three short works he had sent from his fastness, attacking the mass and vows of priesthood. Luther persuaded him to allow their publication, but on returning to the Wartburg wrote to his parishioners warning them against carrying through reforms by violent methods.[1] Revolts, he wrote, bring no improvement; the people must wait till the governments move to reform; if these will not reform, the people must wait in patience, trusting in God's will. Luther's chief solace is an assurance that a judgment of God will visit the earth. The astrologers foretell a great calamity: God grant, he says, that it be the Last Judgment.

This was cold comfort to the zealous followers of Luther, who felt that souls were being lost and their

[1] *Eine treue Vermahnung an alle Christen, sich zu hüten vor Aufruhr und Empörung*, 1522, Vol. VIII.

doctrine injured by the persistence in Wittenberg itself of rites which Luther had condemned. Carlstadt, an enthusiastic reformer, became the leader of the more fiery spirits. Towards the end of the year, he promised to administer the sacrament of communion in both forms to all who came on the following New Year's day. A protest was sent off to the Elector, not merely on theological grounds, but also, and chiefly, because the innovation came from the people and not from the authorities. In haste Carlstadt forestalled the expected prohibition and administered both forms of the sacrament to the congregation on Christmas day. This was repeated several times. The Augustinian monks took a step further by burning the images in their church and taking away the altars, burning also the oil reserved for extreme unction. This example was followed in several churches in the neighbourhood of Wittenberg; a general offensive was set up against ceremonial; a death-blow was struck at monastic life. But a system of welfare had to be devised to take the place of the charitable institutions of the Church, and ordinances for communal life were drawn up. The various funds of the churches which had been devoted to ceremonies such as the Mass were put into a common chest, out of which the poor were granted money for their sustenance and for the education of their children, and indigent workers were given loans free of interest. Beggars were not suffered. These ordinances were approved by the council of University and town, much against the will of the majority; though actually they indicated no radical reform, nothing touching the form of society, but merely regularised charity, and defined the responsibility of the community towards those of its members who were ready to work. One or two violent acts were the result of this change, and the Electoral Government was highly displeased. Disturbing complaints reached it, too, concerning the lack of order in the Church services, there being no order common to two churches. An ostentatious avoidance of confession and infringement of the Lenten fast were further characteristics of the reformers, who, as was complained, seemed to set their whole righteousness in the breaking of the ordinances of the Church.

But though these actions seemed to be merely the realisation of Luther's teaching, it soon became apparent that leaders like Carlstadt were developing a doctrine of a slightly different kind, similar to that of certain men who, exiled from their native town Zwickau, took up their abode at Wittenberg at this time. Zwickau was a prosperous weaving town in Saxony, not far from the Bohemian border, where earlier Hussite refugees had fled. Owing to its considerable trade, the weaving production was in the hands of large merchants, and a definite split had taken place between the mass of small producers and journeymen, and the patriciate and merchants. Amongst the former an anti-clerical party had formed which adopted many of the Hussite doctrines, especially that concerning the immediacy of the relationship between the individual and God. Thomas Münzer [1] had been for a short time pastor at the church in which heretics congregated, and conventicles had been formed at which anyone possessed of the Holy Ghost would speak of the truths of religion. In 1521 it had come to a clash between these levelling tendencies and the traditionalism of the patriciate, and the leaders of the enthusiasts, as they were called (*Schwärmgeister*), were expelled from the town. Many went to Wittenberg, confident of a good reception in the stronghold of anti-clericalism. In Luther's absence no one of his adherents could clearly distinguish between his and the Zwickau doctrines. The enthusiasts laid all weight, as he seemed to do, on immediate heavenly inspiration. On divinely inspired interpretation of the Bible they founded their opposition to the Papacy. They said that certain from their midst were called to be apostles of the true religion. They showed a close acquaintance with the Bible, and were especially fond of the Old Testament and the prophetic books—they themselves indulged a great deal in visions and prophecies, whence they received the name of " prophets." As far as doctrine went, they advanced a little on Luther's teaching by opposing infant baptism; for they said, in complete accordance with Luther's principles, that what is valuable in a sacrament are the faith and inward participation of the individual, not the ceremony; and in infant baptism the child itself takes, of course, no voluntary part.

[1] See also Chap. V.

Melanchthon, who could be considered as Luther's representative at Wittenberg, was impressed by the purity of the doctrine of the enthusiasts, and could find no blemish in it. He communicated their doings and sayings to Luther. It is true he was disturbed in some ways. The beliefs of the enthusiasts caused a different attitude in them from that induced in Luther. The latter had changed nothing in his priestly and parochial duties; but the prophets neglected all worldly affairs, and gave themselves over to the cultivation of religious feeling, to visions and prophecies, and to preaching a general revolution. Along with other reforms founded on an evangelical point of view, they also insisted on obedience to the Mosaic Law, particularly where the latter came into contact with the established order of their time. And further, their conviction that they were in direct contact with God led them to believe themselves justified in the use of force to realise their doctrines in the world, and to favour passages from the Old Testament which exhorted to the extermination of the wicked. They told Melanchthon how in visions the archangel Gabriel had promised one of their number he should sit on his throne, how God had promised another the approaching destruction of the oppressors and Godless. It was disturbing, too, to Melanchthon that the leadership of the reform should go over from Luther to these mainly uneducated weavers, who were prone to broach the question of secular as well as ecclesiastical oppression. Carlstadt, on the other hand, was of one mind with the prophets. He had already appealed to mass-feeling to carry out reforms. It was but a further step for him to proclaim that religion was the affair of the simple-minded. This learned and subtle doctor went round to the common folk asking them their opinion of biblical passages; the Eucharist was administered to children of ten and eleven years of age; learning and thought were considered antagonistic to true religion, and the pious were summoned to take their children away from the schools. With this went a neglect of priestly and pastoral duties, the moribund died unheeded, the sick languished untended.

The Elector was greatly troubled over these innovations and tendencies, the way to which was so unconstitutional and struck across the authority of his reliable, peace-loving subjects who sat in town council and University senate. He did not quite know how to act, however, since he knew that Luther's cause was his, and yet could not see where the innovators differed from Luther. So he let matters go, recommending that his subjects should act with deliberation and in consultation with other Universities. His difficulties were increased when the Bishop of Meissen, supported by the Bishop of Merseburg, asked leave of him to send preachers into Wittenberg to recover the people from their patent errors. If the Imperial Government (the *Reichsregiment*, representing Charles during his absence from Germany) pressed on this request, Frederick could not refuse without declaring open defiance to the imperial authority; and at this time he was far from wishing this. Especially he did not wish to take so drastic a step for the sake of unruly prophets who had no notion of government or of reasons of State. Fortunately, at this moment Luther stepped in.

Luther had received the accounts of the activities of the enthusiasts without agitation. He waited for time to test whether their claims to divine inspiration were justified. What they said was from God, he said, might equally well be of the devil; and in their doctrines and way of life he found no signs of any peculiar godliness. In their repudiation of the sacrament of infant baptism, however, he found great evil and danger. The faith of the assembled congregation, he said, has power to make this sacrament efficacious for the unconscious child. Luther was here abandoning his main principle, by means of which he had destroyed so much of the papal edifice —that only the faith of the participant makes sacraments efficacious—and though he always stood by the doctrine of infant baptism, he never succeeded in justifying it. It was the first step backward from his revolutionary programme. And the cause of this retreat was very deep-lying: he feared the class of men who advanced this theory, he feared the too-consequent application of his theories because it would lead to the destruction of any system, he feared to lose his authoritarian position; the doctrines he had preached he had understood only in a certain sense and with an eye to a particular interpretation, which he was now with all his might to force on men.

The attitude of his own flock at Wittenberg was an especial grief to him. He wished to visit the town, but refrained for the moment from doing so at the request of Spalatin and the Elector, and wrote a pastoral letter to the community. In it he said he had seen with dismay the importance his friends attributed to insignificant rites and the lack of charity they showed to their neighbours. His trouble grew, and in spite of the remonstrances of his prince he travelled to Wittenberg in order to put matters to rights, daring to take the step because he knew he would save the cause of the Elector with his own. Immediately, on each of eight successive days, he preached publicly on the innovations. On the whole he did not bring into question the rightness of the ideas, but sharply censured the methods employed. The Word, persuasion, should effect the change, not violence. He summed up his criticism in the words: " For it has taken place in wickedness, without any order, with injury to one's neighbour . . . one should first have earnestly pondered it in prayer and have taken counsel with the rulers, so would one have known that it was from God." Furthermore, one should have asked for his advice. The importance of this statement of policy is that Luther defines his method of reform. In *To the Christian Nobility* he had made a general, vague appeal to the secular powers to reform the Church, but had not said what steps should be taken; he had shirked the positive question in the belief that the Day of Judgment was at hand. Now, however, he stated that no action should take place without the assent of the rulers, implying at the same time that no change should take place in the order of temporal society. This he had prepared for in his *Freedom of a Christian*, where he had drawn a sharp division between religious and secular affairs and had left all power in the secular sphere to the overlords. But, since doctrines could be deduced from the Bible which were politically subversive, he found it necessary to fashion an authority which would effectively affirm his point of view. At this point in his struggles he could rely on his own prestige, then at its highest point, and so he called to his listeners: " Follow me, I have never led you wrong; I was the first whom God set on this plan; I cannot escape God, but must remain as long as it is well-pleasing in His sight; it was I also to whom God first gave the revelation to preach and publish His Word. . . ." It is an appeal to men to accept unquestioningly Luther's leadership.

Luther carried the day. The Conservative Party, the Town Council and the University, as also Melanchthon and the mass of the middle class, who had looked on with mixed feelings at the disturbance of the social order, welcomed him as a saviour. Chains were laid on popular enthusiasm, though most of the innovations which had been carried through were accepted. The administration of confiscated revenue was taken out of the hands of the innovators and put into those of the secular authorities, it being understood that the Town Council would have a policy well-pleasing to the Elector. Carlstadt was silenced for a time, a reply he wrote to Luther's dogmatic injunctions being suppressed before it was printed, by order of the University. Though Luther had not directly attacked the doctrines of the enthusiasts in his sermons, he had several conversations with their leaders, and let them know that he considered that everything they said which was not borne out by Holy Scripture was of the devil. Very soon they quietly left Wittenberg.

For some time the reform movement continued under the aegis of Luther. Where a bold lead had been given by the more violent spirits he did not fear to follow, with the modification that the form of the changes should be controlled by the secular authorities. Confiscations of Church property were carried out by lords or town councils (these were, of course, always the more settled, the richer part of the community.)[1] In most cases the poorer section of the community did not profit by the changes, for rarely was an adequate share of the newly acquired funds put by for communal purposes—charities, schools, etc. Often, indeed, sharp controversies rose between the religious congregations and the secular communities. But there was the appearance of radical reform in the superficial changes in ceremonial and

[1] As Luther wrote (July 1524): " It is not our business to attack the monasteries, but to draw hearts away from them. *When then churches and monasteries are lying deserted, let the reigning princes do with them as they please.*" (Cf. K. Kautsky, *Communism in Central Europe,* p. 128.)

custom. Many services were done away with.
Images were removed—though Luther never advocated their destruction, saying that while they
should not be adored, yet it was an aid to piety to
see illustrations of sacred events. Monks and nuns
left their cloisters and abandoned their vows of
celibacy. Carlstadt and Münzer were two of the
first priests to take wives. But still Luther made no
attempt to reorganise the Church, being content to
leave matters to the wisdom of the secular masters,
and defining the relationship between Church and
State no further than he had done in the *Freedom of
a Christian*. He believed people would accept his
new orthodoxy, which would have meant their quiet
submission to their rulers.

A revolt against his dogma was the necessary consequence of a widespread dissatisfaction with the
social order Luther maintained. Carlstadt, who
was still lecturing on the Gospel, took a piece of land
near Wittenberg. There he lived with his wife as
a peasant, being called " neighbour Andrew," and
tried to lead a life more in harmony with Gospel
teaching than his former academic environment had
allowed—though he continued to draw his profes-
sorial salary. And he entered into correspondence
with Münzer, the most striking and fearless figure in
the prophet-movement. This man was inspired
equally by religious and social motives, and laid the
greatest accent on those biblical sayings which deal
with the social implications of religion. He cited
Psalm v. : " Whoever taketh honours and goods into

possession will be eternally lost to God at the last."
Like all the " prophets," he gave the voice of inward
conviction much more validity than did Luther, and
would accept only those teachings of the Bible which
were supported by inward revelation, thus openly
defining a selective principle which Luther followed
without confessing to it. He encouraged the study
of the Old as well as the New Testament, and came
to such doctrines as: that the godless have no right
to live except in so far as they are permitted by the
elect. After his banishment from Zwickau, Münzer
travelled over a good part of Germany, and enter-
tained connexions with centres of discontent in
various parts of the country. After some time he was
made preacher at the townlet of Allstedt in Thüringia,
where he carried out a reform of the Church.

What distinguished Münzer most clearly from
Luther was his advocacy, on Christian principle, of
social as well as ecclesiastical reforms; and his consequent advocacy of the use of force. The dictates of
the Bible were clear enough for him, and anyone
who refused to obey them made himself liable to
punishment. In his own parish the common people
decided on the immediate reformation of the Church.
But not only that: to some extent a communism of
goods was introduced. Münzer and his adherents
declared not only that the principle of lending at
interest was against the word of God, in which
Luther agreed with him, but also that the payment of interest by the debtor constituted a crime
against sacred law. If this decision had been

generally carried out, it would have created a great turmoil in the whole of the society of the day, and not least in circles which supported Lutheranism. Münzer's community felt its antagonism to the existing order, and went so far on one occasion, when officers of the Elector of Saxony came to arrest one of their number for some delict, as to arm in his defence and refuse obedience to the ruler of the land. A league was formed, in which Münzer and Pfeiffer, the preacher at the free imperial city of Mülhausen, were the leading spirits. Their explicit aim was the destruction of all oppressors of the poor and godly, both lay and ecclesiastical, and the levelling of property, and they were determined, if the princes opposed their plans, to use force to achieve them. Their league, which in the towns defended the interests of the small masters and journeymen, was founded in the country on the needs of the peasants and agricultural workers (those who cultivated other than food-products, such as wood, etc.) and of the mining population, which was considerable in Saxony, and which, through the use of machines, was in some degree becoming proletarianised. Münzer was the most radical head among the educated leaders. He saw the absolute antagonism between his and Luther's evangelicalism, and the consequent inevitability of war to the bitter end. The others accompanied him with a radical theology. Anabaptism became a doctrine of the league, and Carlstadt developed a new interpretation of the sacrament of communion which rejected the supernaturalistic belief of Luther in favour of the more rational doctrine that the bread and wine were merely symbols of Christ.

The Elector and Duke George of Saxony (not electoral Saxony) visited Allstedt, and, to the great displeasure of Luther, allowed Münzer to preach before them. Münzer was not intimidated, and called on them to leave their ways and destroy the godless by force. Luther now took alarm, and in a violent work *Against the Spirit of Revolt*,[1] urged the Elector to take action against these men who themselves incited to force. In the spirit of an earlier work *On Secular Overlordship*,[2] he repeated that force should not be used to make men pious, but to protect men from the attacks of the impious; and that these monsters in Allstedt were overthrowing the peace of the country. Under the influence of this work the richer classes in Allstedt, who had formerly controlled the town and had suffered under the reforms, plucked up courage and were successful in turning Münzer out of the town and in restoring the old order. He fled to his confederate in Mülhausen, where he was out of the jurisdiction of the Saxon lord. Under the spur of his agitation Mülhausen was reformed, though no thorough communisation was carried out and the power of the hereditary patriciate was not broken. Pfeiffer seems to have satisfied himself with certain reforms in favour of the

[1] *Ein Brief an die Fürsten zu Sachsen von dem aufrührerischen Geist*, 1524, Vol. XV.
[2] *Von weltlicher Oberkeit, wie weit man ihr Gehorsam schuldig sei*, 1523, Vol. XI.

exploited craftsmen. After a little while, the conservative forces reasserted themselves, and Münzer and Pfeiffer were expelled. They went into exile, wandering over the southern parts of Germany, spreading their doctrines as they went, and meeting in most places with the sympathy of the lower classes. Luther followed them with scourging writings. With Carlstadt Luther was more lenient, treating him as an erring sheep, and attempting to win him back. On the interpretation of the communion Carlstadt was, however, adamant, and he too was banished. In South Germany, particularly in Strasburg, he also found many adherents. He joined forces with Zwinglianism, which adopted his doctrine and which, though, like Lutheranism, oppressing anabaptists and levellers, differed from it by its more republican spirit. The more radical and independent interpretation of the Bible was accompanied here too by a radical opposition to the overlords, in particular to the Emperor. And it is significant that not for the most urgent reasons of expediency could Luther bring himself to a league with the followers of Zwingli, owing to their attitude to the authority of the Bible; though for the sake of his overlords he made great concessions away from Christian doctrine.

Right to the end Luther conserved an irreconcilable hatred towards the anabaptists. In the period 1528–1530 he wrote many works against them. His chief arguments were that nowhere in the Bible was the baptism of children proved to be against God's word; and that to maintain that children are unable to believe is a mere opinion: Christ, indeed, set the child in the midst. The first argument is a complete reversal of his original principle, and could have been used to justify most of the ecclesiastical rites which Luther attacked; the second is sophistical and seems a wilful misunderstanding of Christ's saying. To such contradictions of his own doctrine did Luther's defence of his dogma lead him; political repression of the sects went hand in hand with Luther's sophistry.

Of a more comprehensive importance were the writings in which Luther attempted to distinguish his own evangelicalism from that of the enthusiasts and revolutionaries. In particular, those sermons, preached at the end of the year of the peasants' revolts, 1525, in which he defined the relationship between his Christianity, the Mosaic law, and the established order, reveal the structure of his religion. He recognises the difficulty openly. There are three sorts of law, he says in *How Christians should Fit Themselves to Moses*.[1] One the secular law, where the sword rules; one the spiritual law, which is composed of grace and forgiveness of sins; and another, midway between the other two, which the Jews created, where divine commands and external ceremonies rule, and which lays down how man shall behave towards God and man. Luther does not doubt that this law was given to Moses by God immediately; rather he stresses this in the Sermon on the nine-

---

[1] *Ein Unterrichtung, wie sich die Christen in Mosen sollen schicken,* 1526, Vol. XVI.

teenth and twentieth chapters of Exodus; [1] but it is from this law that the Christian law has delivered us. The law of Moses, he repeats several times, was binding for the Jews, just as the Roman law, or the Mirror of the Saxons (*sächsischer Spiegel*, the common law of the Saxon peoples), was binding for the Romans and Saxons. But it has no merit for or power over other peoples, over the Gentiles. Many points in Mosaic law are still valid. Not, however, because they are the commands of God, but because they are inherent in all natural law, because they are "written in the human heart," as, for instance, the belief in one God, the condemnation of adultery, etc.

It is therefore wrong for Christians to prefer the law of Moses to the law they find in their native country. But in making this conclusion Luther has taken away the divine element from Moses' law and has contradicted his own statement that Mosaic law was a mid-way thing between secular law and Christian law. He tries to cover over this confusion by pointing out the moral value of Mosaic law in its exposition of the rewards and punishments following on acceptance of and opposition to God's commands, and by his insistence that the law was given to Moses by God Himself. But, in spite of this, he reiterates that the Mosaic law must give way before the commands of the existing powers, and that natural law, though written in the heart by God, is valuable only as a system of constraint: that there is no merit in accomplishing any of the commands of this law.

[1] Vol. XVI (Sept. 10, 1525).

But the whole value of the law of Moses, both for the Jews and for the enthusiasts, lay exactly in this: that it differed from secular law in being not a mere system of constraint, but the definition of a mode of life well-pleasing in God's sight. In this way Luther not only destroyed the binding quality of the law of Moses, in particular where it favoured a form of society which was not pleasing to him, but also gave every established order a metaphysical sanction. The rewards and punishments of the law reflect God's judgments, and have an absolute value as forms of justice.

The equivalence of Mosaic and secular law in Luther's eyes is shown clearly in the *Instruction of Visitors to Pastors* of 1528,[1] where, in order to show the necessity of obeying the rulers of the land, Luther adduces out of the Old Testament examples of the punishment of law-breakers. The first example he takes is of a peculiar interest. It is the punishment of Korah, Dathan, and Abiram for their revolt against the autocracy of Moses.[2] These men took exactly the same position towards Moses as did the enthusiasts towards Luther: " Ye (Moses and Aaron) take too much upon you, seeing all the congregation are holy, every one of them, and the Lord is among them: wherefore then lift ye up yourselves above the congregation of the Lord? " This revolt Luther treats as if it were simply a revolt against the secular order. His choice of it shows how he strengthened at the

[1] *Unterricht der Visitatoren an die Pfarrherrn*, Vol. XXVI.
[2] Numbers xvi.

same time the authority of the State and his own authority in theological matters; the two causes were identical. Luther's doctrine is that Christianity consists entirely in the belief in Christ; the substance of Christ's teaching is unimportant: " The Gospel does not teach us what we must do or leave undone, but says: God has done this for you, has made His Son flesh for you, has had Him done to death for you." [1] And the whole moral system, all human institutions have no specific merit, but are to be absolutely respected as being divinely instituted: " For we should fear all earthly law and order as God's will and law. As Solomon says, Proverbs xvi., A divine sentence is in the lips of the king." [2]

This method of confusion whereby Luther retained his authoritative position and strengthened the domination of the secular lords is nowhere more clear than when he attempted to refute the theories of the enthusiasts and levellers, in particular of Carlstadt. The work *Against the Divine Prophets, concerning Images and the Sacrament*,[3] is a ruthless attack on his opponents. In it he identifies without any more ado all attempts at basing religion on the poor and simple-minded with rebellion and conspiracy. He sums up the activity of the iconoclasts as papistry and belief in the efficacy of good works, and includes under this denomination the affectation of peasant's

[1] *Unterrichtung wie sich die Christen in Mosen sollen schicken*, Vol. XVI, p. 367.
[2] *Unterricht der Visitatoren*, Vol. XXVI, p. 211.
[3] *Wider die himmlischen Propheten von den Bildern und Sakrament*, 1525, Vol. XVIII.

garb by Carlstadt. Carlstadt rejoined that he attributed no holiness to peasant's dress in itself, but that Christ had said that the rich would hardly enter the Kingdom of Heaven; also that the existence of the images was a sore peril for simple, misled people. Luther answered this by saying there was no need to remove or destroy images once one had come to the true faith; and quotes the case of the prophet Elisha, who allowed Naaman to pray, with an inward reservation, in the temple of Rimmon. (II Kings, v.)[1] Luther defines love and charity as purely spiritual qualities, while Carlstadt wished to live in their light by entering into the life of the poor and oppressed. Luther states: For Christians there must be a spiritual way of approach, but "for the rough people, for Master Everybody (Herr Omnes, a common term of abuse in Luther's writings for the uneducated and simple) one must set corporally and roughly about the task, and force them with the sword and the law to do and leave undone according to the law, and to be outwardly pious, as wild beasts are kept with chains and cages."[2]

In order to justify his devotion to the rulers, Luther uses in this work the same arguments as in *How Christians should Fit Themselves to Moses*, and their tendenciousness is even more visible than in the later

[1] As Luther had said in the *Vorrede auf die Epistel Sanct Paulus zu den Römern* (1522), he would not have Christians oppose the law. They should change their attitude to the law, and fulfil it, not because it is a pious exercise, but because they are impelled to do so by their own hearts.

[2] *Wider die himmlischen Propheten*, Vol. XVIII, p. 66.

work. The law of Moses is, he repeats, the Jews' Mirror of the Saxons. We must take from it only that which agrees with natural law, *i.e.* with the established law. The only divine element in Moses is to be found in those passages relating to the creation of the world, to the prophecies of Christ's coming, and those illustrating God's grace and terribleness towards His faithful and unfaithful servants. But by including the latter among the evidences of the divine in Moses, Luther is ascribing divinity to all legal judgments; for, since God's judgments, in the books of Moses, are based on the law enunciated by Moses, and since the law of Moses is not more sacred for Luther than any established law, then any legal judgments have a divine quality. Luther's inference is clear. He supports his command that any reform must be instigated and carried out by the rulers by a reference to the institution of rulers by Moses (Exodus xviii.), and identifies the princes of his time with the nominees of God's servant, " able men, such as fear God, men of truth, hating covetousness "! In this work Luther was attacking two things: the doctrine that Christ's teaching was for the simple-minded; and the doctrine that Christ's kingdom was to be realised by force; both being aspects of the same attitude. The former he did not treat explicitly. The latter he refuted by his exposition of the nature of Mosaic law. But from his theory of this law he drew metaphysical sanction for his own political theory and justified his tolerance of the established system.

(b) *The Formation of the Lutheran Church*

In his attitude to the sects, then, Luther showed that he had no wish to found a society which would be ordered according to the dictates of Holy Scripture. When he had said that all men were both lay and spiritual members of the community, and that the Church should not exist separately from the State, he had meant something different. He had first hoped that on receipt of his theological message all men, including the Pope, would be infused with such a religious spirit that institutions would be superfluous. When this hope had burst, he called on the princes to correct the most blatant errors of the Roman Church and on the bishops to reconstruct the Church on a national basis.[1] This would probably have been for him the most natural reform method. There would have been a national church guided by a council of bishops directly responsible for their policy to the national and local governments. The Church would thus have ceased being a foreign and independent power, and could have been quickly brought to heel if it had pursued a policy injurious to the rights of the community as represented by the princes. But few bishops took the side of Luther from the beginning, and fewer still after some of the common people had forcibly taken charge of the reforms. Luther had to devise another solution. It must be noted that his first scheme of reconstruction by no means did away with the idea of a hier-

[1] In *To the Christian Nobility.*

archy; and he later tried to preserve or create a priesthood in spite of his statements that all men are " Co-Christians, co-priests."

The break-up of the Church proceeded apace after the events at Wittenberg in 1521–22, and Luther had to accept this development. In many parts the parishes imposed their will on their former priests, though Luther kept the people in restraint by the doctrine that all confiscated property belonged to the secular authorities. Out of the general chaos caused by this method of reform Luther set himself to fashion an order. In the *Writing to Prague concerning the Institution of Church-servants*,[1] he outlined the method to be followed. Each congregation of believers, each parish, should come together and elect a spiritual head who would be responsible for the services of the Church and the moral duties of a pastor. This election should be ratified by the more influential members of the community (*potiores*). The heads should form themselves into councils, and elect a bishop, with visitors who should attend to the health and vigour of the religious life in the communities. There should be no distinction between lay and spiritual except by office, and any member should have the right to dispute on doctrinal matters with the heads and bishops, as God should inspire him. By this system a sort of priesthood was created of those spiritually gifted, but it was not given any authority in doctrine. Where it was applied, in all congregations many doctrines arose immediately

---

[1] *Schreiben an die böhmischen Landstände*, 1522, Vol. X.

which were not those of Luther, and which he judged erroneous; members too were at loggerheads with one another. No order was brought into the new church, but its dissensions were more clearly revealed. The lack of a means of enforcing the "correct" doctrine was keenly felt. Luther now had recourse to another expedient. He tried to form one or two select congregations of true believers—at Wittenberg and Leisnig—which should provide an example and right line for the rest. He was driven back to the position: "The Gospel is not for all, not yet," and called the many unorthodox swine. In Wittenberg he managed to keep the faith pure, by virtue of his own influence and prestige; but in Leisnig even this scheme failed.[1] There were quarrels between the secular and religious bodies as to control of financial resources. Worse still, the same errors cropped up as elsewhere, there was the same obstinate, unyielding controversy, and there was no means of deciding what was orthodox, and no means of enforcing the right view and exterminating errors. In any case, the idea of a select religious community, specially favoured of God, was inconsistent with the fundamental principles of Luther.

The ultimate form of the Lutheran Church was calculated to counteract the self-government of the congregations. To regularise the various communities, as far as order of services, purity of doctrine, and arrangement of pastoral duties were concerned, a series of visitations was organised from

[1] Cf. p. 215.

Wittenberg, and it was round the arbitration of this central band of visitors that the new Church system formed itself, under Luther's direct supervision. His personal authority counted for much; but he had an even more reliable authority to fall back upon. In the major decisions of his life he had always referred to the Elector, through the medium of Spalatin. Now it became the custom to refer even religious questions to the Elector's Court. Luther did not scruple, on some occasions, when the Lutheranisation of a community was opposed by some of its influential members, to appeal to the Elector to come to the help of the reformers with force. It became impossible for Catholics to live in the reformed lands. Luther could influence the censorship. Suits concerning marriages, tithes, delicts against secular and ecclesiastical law, affairs of church discipline were dealt with by the Elector's Court. The new system was summed up in the *Instruction of Visitors to the Pastors* of 1527.[1] Melanchthon had already stated that it was the duty of the secular overlord to preserve discipline in matters of cult and orthodoxy, and this " Instruction " defined the range of subjects which should come under his control. Officials, town-councillors, noble patrons of courts of law, should punish all things which are not to be suffered among Christians, such as frivolous swearing and taking the name of God in vain, drunkenness, gaming, idleness, frivolous talk on matters touching faith (an article which was often

[1] Vol. XXVI.

turned against sectarians, in particular the anabaptists), adultery, fornication, disobedience of
children towards their parents, in particular over
the question of marriage. Similarly, false doctrines,
neglect of attendance at church, and disturbance of
the Church service were to be punished.

Luther had in the beginning stated as a principle
that the use of force to advance the faith, even to
protect the faithful, was not justified. This attitude
had won him a great many adherents out of the ranks
of the Conservative classes. Now, when faced by
the divisions in his own supporters, he allowed and
implored the secular authorities to exercise the most
exact control over religious affairs, even to interfere
in matters of doctrine. He and his Elector tried to
re-introduce the ecclesiastical ban as a punishment
for religious misdemeanours. Indeed, Melanchthon
wrote that it was the first duty of the most eminent
member of the Church, *i.e.* the lord of the land, to
take care that " errors are extirpated and consciences
purified." Together with this went a separation of
the clergy from the common people. In his writings
on education [1] Luther always insisted on the need
of producing learned priests and jurists, both being
necessary for the health of the community. The
jurists he often found occasion to fulminate against,
as being a class which served the princes against the
interests of the people; and the clergy tended also
to develop class nature and class interests. Luther
more and more considered his priesthood as a pecu-

[1] See Chap. VII.

liarly chosen and favoured class, raised high above the level of other men. In 1530 he wrote: " As highly as eternal life surpasses this temporal life, so much does the office of the preacher surpass all secular office."[1] He was thus affirming the distinction between priest and layman which he had formerly most violently and successfully attacked. It is significant that, on the order of the Protestant Margrave of Brandenburg, an edition of the papal decretals was published in 1530, to which Luther attached a preface.[2]

In 1539 the connexion between Church and State, between theologians and secular authority, was finally established by the institution of Consistorial Councils. These were composed of two theologians and two jurists, all nominated by the head of the State. The consistory controlled dogma and morals. It instituted regular visitations of parishes at which the secular councillors should be examined concerning the behaviour of the priests, and the priests concerning that of their flock; an adequate method of strengthening the power of the central authority. It had in its power all the machinery of the State, police, law-courts, etc. It could impose not only fines and imprisonment, but also complete social boycott, i.e. the withdrawal of civic rights and the prohibition of industrial and commercial activity —the exact counterpart of the papal ban. This legis-

[1] *Predigt, dass man Kinder zur Schule halten solle*, Vol. XXX, ii, p. 554.
[2] Vol. XXX, ii, pp. 215 ff.

lation applied to delicts in the sphere of religion which Luther had proclaimed, in the years up to 1521, as free to the individual. And while such delicts had been formerly dealt with by a purely ecclesiastical court, they were now in the hands of a court nominated by the lord of the land, whose will was paramount. Luther had freed religion from one captivity to subject it to another enslavement.[1]

Luther, then, who had claimed to set the individual in a new and immediate relationship with God, had in the final form of his reform erected a new hierarchy and a new orthodoxy. Did he acquiesce unwillingly in this development, seeing that it was necessary in order to secure certain fundamental reforms, or was it his undefined intention from the beginning? It is true that he had repeatedly asserted the right of each individual to decide on matters of doctrine and on the interpretation of the Bible, and that he now denied this right; but in what connexion did this final doctrine of his arise, and in what connexion does it stand to the rest of Luther's doctrine? His central theological doctrine, that of the powerlessness of man to earn divine grace and of the inefficacy of ecclesiastical penances, he had evolved oblivious of the possibility of the abolition of the Church. He thought that it could be accepted within the ecclesiastical system, *i.e.* that it would not affect the Church as an institution and would take its place in the dog-

---

[1] For an example of Lutheran legislation pushed to its extreme see the scheme drawn up by his adherent, Eberlin von Günzburg, translated in Schapiro, *op. cit.*, pp. 118–25.

matic system. It was only when he was brought up against the obstinate opposition of the Papacy that Luther pressed for the right of the individual to interpret Holy Scripture. This latter doctrine was essentially a polemical weapon. And always there was in his mind the fundamental belief in an orthodoxy. He always thought that on matters of faith a council of the Church should decide, which is equivalent to believing that there is a right and wrong faith. Similarly, though he claimed the right of the common man to decide on matters of religion, he never contemplated doing away with the learned priesthood, and was conscious that a priesthood was necessary. Thus, though there are formal contradictions between his earlier and later attitude, a deeper investigation shows that one consistent intention inspired his actions.

From the beginning Luther's heaviest attacks on the Church were on the score of its being an alien power existing side by side with the secular powers. His aim was to make of Church and State a unity. To this end, he insisted on a sharp distinction between natural and divine law. The former governs all secular matters, and its best representative is equity, the latter governs the soul. The Church, which is the community of all souls, is free of secular control and responsible only before God; but divine law is incomprehensible to man and cannot be formulated. The papal Church had organised itself in a hierarchy according to natural law; this, however, was wrong, said Luther, for it is not a secular organisation, and does not need a head. Religion is purely a matter for the individual soul. Luther could so confidently proclaim this principle because when he did so the disruption of the Catholic Church had not yet begun nor was envisaged. After the change of heart which the acceptance of his own true doctrine would induce, the Church would still go on existing as an institution, in order to preach true doctrine and to advocate proper morality; but it would not claim any secular identity, and would merely be an organisation to prevent men from falling into error. Luther never intended that the Church should cease to be, but only that it should have a character not inimical to the secular interests of its members. And in so far as the Church has any outward representation, it is subject to natural law —that is, is subject to the existing law of the land. Its task is, then, to sustain that order whereby it exists. By this means did Luther bring Church and State into a unity, though it meant that the Church was subservient to the State.

Luther's clinging to the dogmatic view of theology was equivalent to acceptance of the idea of a hierarchy. He abhorred and fought vehemently against all variations of his doctrines. This could be explained psychologically as arising from his will to keep the leadership of the movement in his own hands; but the cause lies far deeper than this. Why should he have felt that there was so great a need of order in doctrine? The obvious answer is that when he relaxed control his doctrines were adapted from

religious matters to certain social interests. He
wished to remain a theologian pure and simple.
But Luther continually showed that, far from being
uninterested in social questions, he had a very clear
idea of what was socially desirable. Even though
he at times approved of the actions carried out by
popular will, he always disapproved of this method
of action. Reforms, he said, must be carried out by
the natural rulers—princes, nobles, or, in the cities,
town-councillors—not by the plebs, by "Master
Omnes"; and for the sake of this principle he was
willing that his proposed reforms should be infinitely
delayed and many souls irrevocably lost thereby. His
dogmatic conception of religion, his insistence on the
incontrovertible authority of his own formulations
was the metaphysical aspect of his social attitude.

But he was not an authoritarian in the sense that a
medieval theologian was an authoritarian. He was
not afraid of striking at times an individualistic attitude, though of course with inward reservations.
His doctrine did not support authority for its own
sake, and was the cause of the disruption of traditional authority; as a result his social thought, like
his theology, seems to be of an expediential nature.
The cause of this reveals the basis of his whole attitude. Luther's moral doctrine is consistently that
of the settled middle-class, who, while striving for a
greater measure of freedom in economic affairs,
still depended for their prosperity on the continuance
of the social order. Their chief enemies were the
Papacy, who imposed heavy dues on them and took

the wealth of their customers out of their locality; the Empire, which imposed tasks on them and their country which had no relation to their immediate prosperity; the monopolist merchants and the international bankers, who threatened them with bankruptcy: and the lower classes of artisans, journeymen, peasants, who demanded a larger share in profits and civic government. The first and last of these enemies created theologies to represent their needs, and it was the task of the middle class to oppose these theologies with one of its own. This was Luther's. But it could not enforce itself without political backing. Obviously on many points the interests of this bourgeoisie were not identical with those of the absolutist, particularist princes, but they had common antagonisms. For this reason the bourgeoisie accepted the help of the princes and gave them their support. They made a compromise with them, and after affirming a new order with the aid of revolutionary principles, they proclaimed the new order sacred, and then modified the principles. Order, maintained by absolute power, was necessary for them; and the absolutism which coincided with the greatest number of their interests was that of the princes. It is to be noticed that the theological system of Calvin and Zwingli, which was introduced in a country where the aristocracy was weak and the bourgeoisie strong, was able to be much more of a logical deduction from its first revolutionary principles than Luther's. But in all cases the old principle of dogma had to be restored in order to assert the inviolability of the existing order, in order to protect a particular class, whose morality was considered highest and whose interests were thought sacred. Against the interests of this class Luther never acted, and the further history of his major decisions will show how, from this point of view, his thought was perfectly consequent.

CHAPTER V

THE EVOLUTION OF LUTHER'S POLITICAL THEORY

(a) *Luther and the Peasant Risings*

THE last chapter showed how Luther came step by step to a realisation of his conception of the Church, and how he subordinated religion to the existing political order. Just as he wished at first to accept many of the elements of the papal Church and to make few changes, so with regard to the political system of his time he was reluctant to plan out a new order. His doctrine was that he, as a theologian, had no right to interfere in the secular sphere. But as an effect of his religious reform, parties rose for and against him, troubles were caused among the political powers. His doctrinal party became more closely identified with a small political party, and he himself, as its conscience, had to make decisions concerning action to be taken. He had to declare why he supported a certain party. At first he could accept the whole structure of the Empire because he hoped that all its members, from the Emperor to the free cities, would take his side against the Papacy. Thus he would not sanction the use of force or any division within the ranks of the secular powers; and also he made no distinction between the powers who had interests similar to those of his class and those who had not. He saw in the class of Imperial Knights a possible ally, and was distressed by their suppression by the territorial princes; though actually they were against any order which would strengthen the security and power of the towns and bourgeoisie, as they were against Papacy, Empire, and princes. As, however, with the partial success of his reform its sociological implications became clear, antagonistic parties crystallised out. Of these the most important were the peasants and lower classes in the towns, and the party of authority round the Emperor. The struggle with the former is best dealt with first, as it consolidated Luther's party for its later struggle with the Emperor.

The history of medieval Europe is marked by sporadic outbreaks of the peasantry, the common characteristic of which was the combination of demands for social and ecclesiastical reforms. Oppressed by princes, knights, burghers, and Church, they rose and demanded, and sometimes carried through, the abolition of private ownership, the communisation of wealth and rights, and the breakdown of clericalism, basing all their claims on primitive Christian doctrine. They were the ready material for all religious reformers, such as Wiclif, and often proved a source of embarrassment to them because of the radicalness of their aims. They had much the same economic antagonisms as the lower strata in the towns, who generally joined with them in their revolt against authority; though this alliance was unsure, since their ultimate ends were dissimilar, and it often happened that at a certain moment, after a certain amount of success, the town-workers would quit the common cause for a partial settlement.

During the fifteenth century the position of the peasants grew considerably worse. The cost of living increased and hit them hardest, while in the towns luxuries became more common. The country was treated as a colonial area by the town-guilds, who attempted to effect a monopoly of production and trade. The peasants, always badly organised, had no answer to this exploitation. The developing power of the towns hit the Imperial Knights too, who, having by this time lost their military importance, had no power of resistance; and the knights were forced, for sheer self-preservation, to wring from their serfs all the profit possible.[1] Since the rights of the peasants were mainly unwritten, handed down by oral tradition, they were easily overriden by the bold and unscrupulous overlords. The larger princes went to work to deprive the peasants of their rights in a more subtle and effective way. In spite of constant opposition from moralists and theologians, there was a general process, from the end of the fifteenth century, of replacement of the old native law by Roman law. It is interesting that in this period of the Renaissance the introduc-

[1] See Lamprecht, *op. cit.*

tion of Roman law was opposed by the humanists, the admirers of Rome, as a class.[1] Instead of the old courts of law, where the peasant had been judged by his peers and had pleaded his case himself, with very little cost, new courts were instituted with learned judges, where the peasant had to be represented by a lawyer with a knowledge of subtleties. Lawsuits were dragged out in length, and the lawyers fleeced their clients. But the new system brought not merely a different method of litigation. It changed the very principles of society. In Roman law the prince is considered the absolute head of his land, a position the fief-holders of the German empire could not claim by virtue of native German law. And further, in place of the complicated rights of the various classes of peasants— such who held their land for a period of time, or as an inheritance, under varying conditions of dues and forced services; besides also the serfs proper (*Leibeignen*)—it substituted the concept of the peasant in the Roman Empire, which was that of the slave.[2] The relation between prince and peasant was fundamentally revised through the introduction of the new law.

[1] This is a sign of the true meaning of the Renaissance. The revolutionary political situation created an attitude which would sanction and encourage the break-up of traditional authority. When, however, the new order had affirmed itself, dogmatism again became necessary, and the freedom of thought which had been learnt from the Ancients was again enchained.

[2] Thus Frederick the Victorious, Elector of the Palatinate, won a decision from a Roman jurist giving him supreme rights over all common lands in his territories. See Schapiro, *op. cit.*, p. 46, for the method of introduction of the Roman law.

The position of the lower classes in the towns had also grown considerably worse towards the end of the fifteenth century. The government of the towns, as the control of the guilds, was in the hands of an almost hereditary class of burghers, who formed a patriciate. The powerful merchants were able, through the Verlag system, to control production and prices, and to reduce the producers over some areas practically to the status of a proletariat. The masters in the guilds made entry into the guilds almost impossible by increasing money-charges and by imposing complicated laws governing the preparation of the masterpiece. The division of labour, which was already fairly advanced in many industries, including the weaving, printing, mining, and paper-making industries, made mastership increasingly difficult of attainment and created the beginnings of a proletariat.[1] Thus there was in the towns, as in the country, a large class of oppressed workers without a share in the government and with acute grievances, forced to resort to violent methods if they wished to gain justice.

There were several outbreaks of the peasantry at the beginning of the sixteenth century before Luther's reform affirmed itself. In Alsace the Bundschuh (Shoe League, from the shoe that was used as its emblem) had been organised. Its aims were: to cancel all debts, to reduce tolls and taxes, to replace the imperial court of law with a native

[1] Cf. H. Hauser, *Les débuts du Capitalisme*, pp. 8 ff., and Lamprecht, *op. cit.*

one, to control the income of the priests, to destroy
the usurious Jews, to do away with auricular confession—a confused programme which represents
the interests of town-traders as well as those of the
peasantry. The League was crushed with terrible
severity before it was properly organised, many
members being maimed. In spite of this check,
plotting went on, and outbreaks occurred on the
upper Rhine. The Arme Conrad (poor comrade)
was organised in Swabia, where the Duke, Ulrich
of Württemberg, oppressed his subjects ruthlessly.
This rising was more successful, and for a time the
Duke had to retreat with his forces. The insurgents,
supported by some of the populace, occupied some
towns. But the Duke gained over the burghers by
granting their demands, and they renounced their
revolutionary opposition. Being then strong enough,
Ulrich scattered the peasant bands, treating the
insurgents with great ferocity; then he turned his
attention to the townsfolk, and withdrew the privileges he had been forced to yield. This rising and
its course shows the two principles controlling any
such rising of the common people in this period:
the first, that while the peasants and the lower
classes of townsfolk could combine against oppression,
the difference in their final aims made a betrayal
of the former probable after a certain measure of
success was won; and secondly, that while the local
knights and townships could be overwhelmed by
the undisciplined but large and vigorous forces of
the rebels, the princes could successfully withstand

them. And only in Switzerland were the peasants able to gain lasting concessions, because there there were no large principalities.

The peasant rising of 1524–25 stood under a slightly different constellation from those preceding it. The traditional evangelicalism of the peasants was stirred by the successful revolt against clericalism in Wittenberg and by the belief that Luther's doctrine was based on the Gospel. The peasants were not subtle theologians. They did not distinguish between Christ's own doctrine and Paulinism. They expected that social reforms would now be carried out and certain rights granted or restored to them, merely because the new spirit had conquered. Through the preaching and agitation of the extremists whom Luther had ejected from Saxony, they knew of the attempts at building up Christ's kingdom on earth, and saw that much could be done by vigorous action. On the whole, however, the peasants were not capable of such a bold analysis of society as Münzer had made, and were content at first to beg their masters for improvements.

By October 1524 meetings and disturbances among the peasants in South-west Germany and Swabia were common. Luther heard of the protests and hoped they would be a lesson to the lords for their godless conduct. The peasants went systematically to work, and in Upper Swabia was drawn up a declaration of Twelve Articles in which their demands were formulated.[1] They were extremely

---

[1] The Twelve Articles are printed in full, in English trans-

reasonable and moderate in tone and content, and ran to this effect. First, the peasants demanded the right of electing their own priests to preach them the Gospel, whom they should have the right to depose. Second, the great tithe, that on grain, should be divided between the priest, according to his need, and the poor; the little tithes, those on fruit, vegetables, and livestock, they refused to give, " for the Lord created cattle for the free use of man." Third, serfdom should be abolished " unless it be shown us from the Gospel that we are serfs." Fourth, rights of fishing and shooting, belonging to the lords, must be proved to have been purchased from the community or else surrendered—here the peasants reckoned by the native principle that the land belonged to the people originally, while the law of the lords considered it originally their own property; the peasants protested also against the harm done to their crops by huntsmen. Fifth, the peasants complained about the enclosures of communal forests, through which they were bereft of firing and of wood for constructional purposes. Sixth, they begged for " gracious consideration " in respect of forced services. Seventh, no more services should be demanded of them without payment. Eighth, rents should be re-valuated. Ninth, the native German law should be maintained in face of the new Roman law which was being introduced.

lation, in Schapiro, *op cit.*, pp. 137–42. There were many such manifestos at the time, but these articles were representative of the aims of the greatest mass of peasants.

Tenth, enclosures of pasture-lands should be can-
celled. Eleventh, the peasants complained of the
heaviness of death-dues payable to the lords.[1]
Twelfth, they promised to withdraw any article
which could be proved to advance claims irreconcilable with Holy Scripture. These articles did not
go beyond the historical rights of the peasantry, and
show a clear knowledge of their economic needs.
At the same time, they demonstrate political naivety
in being based on the hope that such reforms would
be carried out by the existing authorities. It may
have been that this naivety was the effect of vague
rumours of the reforms in Wittenberg and of the belief
that radical changes had taken place there. The
Twelve Articles were, indeed, sent to Luther in order
to obtain his advice and enlist his support. He
promptly expressed his attitude in the *Enjoinment to
Peace on the Twelve Articles of the Peasantry in Swabia.*[2]

Though by the time Luther received the Articles
the revolt was already in full swing in certain parts
of the country, he did not know of this, and was
therefore able to treat the matter from a theoretical
and general point of view. He begins by saying
that any rebellion is to be avoided, as it would
overturn worldly rule and God's word together—
no doubt with an eye to the sects. Then, turning
first to the lords and princes, he says, no one is so

---

[1] The lords still had the right to demand from the heirs of
deceased peasants their most valuable heirloom. Later this
became a regular death-tax.

[2] *Ermahnung zum Frieden auf die zwölf Artikel der Bauerschaft in
Schwaben,* 1525, Vol. XVIII.

much to blame for the confusion and discontent on earth as you: you act against Holy Gospel and quarrel among yourselves, while the common people go to ruin. The sword is at your throats; God will punish you, if not through the peasants, then by other means. If only you had acted as I recommended in *To the Christian Nobility*, you would have been spared these revolts. This is sharp language that Luther uses; but methods of reform he leaves in the princes' own hands. He then turns to the peasants, and says: I talk to you as to my dear friends, but you are in grievous error. You have wrongly called yourselves Christians, for you have taken to arms. "Injustice on the part of rulers does not excuse rebellion." If you are Christians you should be content to pray for your cause. Luther then discusses the Twelve Articles. The demand of the peasants to elect their own pastor is, he says, right and proper; if their lords refuse to grant it, they should elect a pastor of their own accord; but they must provide for his sustenance out of their own pockets, for the Church income belongs to the lord and his nominee. If their overlord goes so far as not to tolerate their elected priest in his domains, they shall not protest, but shall leave that land and take refuge elsewhere. Luther refused to allow them any right of discussion on the tithe, which is, he says, entirely a matter for the overlord to decide. As for the article in which they demanded the abolition of serfdom, he says every true Christian is content with his estate; serfs can serve the Lord and win grace as easily as princes; this Luther had established in the *Freedom of a Christian*. On other points Luther refused to give an opinion, saying that they were matters for the jurists, not for a theologian, and censured the peasants for having tried to judge of such matters by reference to the Bible. At the end Luther proposed that a committee should investigate the points raised by the peasants, to be composed of nobles and town-councillors: the peasants were not even to be represented on this committee.

This writing shows that Luther used the principle of the separation of the religious and secular sphere in order to strengthen the power of the authorities. What he proposes is absolute obedience to the rulers. When he said the jurists must decide, he knew it was equivalent to denying any rights to the peasants, for the jurists, as he himself often complained, were abject servants of the princes, and their law was unjust. He recommended the peasants to the Christianity of the lords, and knew that these were hard of heart and would grant nothing. But they were the masters, and for Luther, despite their shortcomings, the right masters. His decision could do nothing but exasperate the peasants and justify in their eyes Münzer's charge that Luther was the slave of the princes; and he added fuel to their rage by fulminating against the wickedness of the princes. With this moral indignation with the princes Luther satisfied his conscience. However, by the time this pamphlet of Luther's was published, events had advanced too far for it to have any effect.

There were two other proclamations of the insurgents which represented wide interests. One was the Letter to the Twelve Articles.[1] This was the manifesto of the extremists who grouped round Münzer. It advocated the complete eradication of the propertied classes, by force if need be. No one should live in anything better than a peasant's cottage. No alliance should be tolerated with the owners of castles, with priests, or religious foundations. The basic principle of this document was that the peasants would be defeated if they relied on half-measures or treaties with any other class, that only the destruction of class distinctions would ensure their permanent victory. It is in accordance with the rest of Münzer's works. He had earlier stated that " all things are common and should be distributed as occasion requires. . . . Any prince, count, or baron who, after being earnestly reminded of this truth, shall be unwilling to accept it, is to be beheaded or hanged." He believed that only extreme measures would give the peasants what they wanted; that hopes for a partial improvement, for a modified reform, were vain. And though he, like all other doctrinaires of the time, fell back on a theology for the sanction of his plan of action— and the theology he constructed, though mainly based on Christ's communistic sayings, was a capri-

[1] " Brief zu den zwölf Artikeln." Published in S. Schreiber, *Der deutsche Bauernkrieg. Gleichzeitige Urkunden*, Vol. II, p. 87.

TITLE-PAGE OF A PAMPHLET OF THOMAS MÜNZER.

Translation—Open exposure of the false belief of the faithless world,
    revealed through the witness of the Gospel according to Luke, to
    recall wretched and miserable Christendom to the thought of
    its errors.

Ezechiel, Chap. 8.

Dear Fellows, let us also dig the hole wider, so that all the world
    may see and comprehend who our great masters are, who so
    blasphemously have made God into a painted manikin.

Jeremiah, Chap. 23.

Thomas Müntzer with the Hammer. Mülhausen, 1524.

cious selection of Old and New Testamentary texts—his analysis of the political situation of the peasantry was penetrating. He wrote: " Behold, at the bottom of all the usury, the thieving, the robbery, are our great lords and masters, who take all creatures for their own, the fishes in the water, the birds in the air, the plants on the earth; all must be theirs. Thereupon they let God's command go abroad among the poor people and say: ' God hath spoken, thou shalt not steal '; but it serves them nothing. And while that from all men, the poor ploughman, the journeyman, and all that lives, they pluck their skin from off them, and their flesh from off their bones; should these transgress against the Most-Holy, they must hang. Thereto ' Amen ' saith Doctor Lügner [= Liar, a term of abuse for Luther]. The masters are themselves the cause that the poor man is their foe. They will not do away with the cause of the rebellion; how can the matter turn out well in the long run? As I say this, so I must be rebellious, come what may."[1] Münzer represented the unifying element in the various ideologies of the insurgents, just as practically his rôle was to force on them the recognition of the necessity of solidarity in action.

The other proclamation published by insurgent elements was that of Wendel Hippler, a town-councillor. It represented the aims of the townsfolk who took part in the rising and accepted the possibility of legal constitutional methods of reform. It

[1] T. Münzer, *Hochverursachte Schutzrede*, Mülhausen, 1524.

asked for the institution of High Courts of Law for
the Empire, where justice should be reliable and
responsible; for the division of secular and ecclesiastical office, so that the Empire should be governed
on purely secular principles; for the abolition of
customs barriers within the Empire,[1] and the
standardisation of money, weights, and measures—
from time to time it was found necessary for rulers
and city corporations to issue illustrated guides of
false and debased coinage with their real value, as
minters often debased their coinage without warning, and there was a good deal of speculation in
currency. Further, this proclamation proposed the
secularisation of all ecclesiastical property, a part to
be given to the lords, the rest to be devoted to the
income of the Empire and to be used to pay its
officials. A system of courts of law was to be
erected, composed of representatives of all estates,
including the municipalities and parishes, and
Roman law should be done away with—one or two
doctors of Roman law could be left in the Universities, where their advice could be sought. The
clergy should be moral shepherds of their flocks
and nothing more, the princes and nobles should
protect the interests of their subjects and behave in
a brotherly fashion to one another, communities

[1] Owing to the many local customs and tolls, trade within
the Empire was greatly hindered. In 1522 the Estates themselves had proposed and made plans for a general simplification
of customs within the Empire and the creation of an imperial
customs barrier; but the plan had come to nothing, owing to
the opposition of small rulers and of the international merchants.

should be organised according to God's word. This programme of Hippler's presents the aims of the smaller tradesfolk, aims which at first sight seem easily attainable.[1] But it is built up on no principle. It does not call in question the right of the princes to be absolute rulers. It asks them to modify their power in favour of the middle class and the Empire. It confounds religious and secular aims in a compromise dictated by class interests; for while Münzer based his religion and his secular order on one and the same principle, Hippler proposed secular reforms which would suit his class, and then added the proviso that communities should organise themselves according to God's Word. If Hippler had had a sufficient backing and could have carried out his proposed reforms, he would have discovered the same contradictions as Luther did. Actually, however, Hippler had no political force to maintain his interests, and his only way of asserting them was to throw in his lot with the revolutionary peasants.

In one place, the Allgäu, where there was no powerful prince, the demands of the peasants as embodied in the Twelve Articles were for the time being conceded. Elsewhere the authorities temporised and looked about for sufficient forces to subdue the arrogance of their subjects. The situation favoured the peasants, for the forces of the

[1] These reform schemes are based largely on the Reformation of the Emperor Sigismund of *ca.* 1437. This had been republished four or five times during 1520–21. See W. Böhm, *Friedrich Reisers Reformation des Kaisers Sigismund.*

Empire were engaged in the war against France, and the princes were unable to collect armies. The peasants became impatient and gathered in bands. They were joined by the riff-raff, out-of-work mercenaries, etc. They saw the impossibility of gaining their aim legally. And soon the whole of South-western Germany was ablaze. They swept across the country, and had no difficulty in sub-duing the isolated knights and religious foundations. In some places they followed Münzer's plan and put all to the sword who refused to accept their creed, burning property. Many knights recognised the necessity of the situation and took arms with the insurgents, hoping at least thus to have a weapon whereby they could bargain to their own profit with the princes. Many of these knights, like Götz von Berlichingen and Florian Geyer, became mili-tary leaders of the peasants; and this policy was so successful that, in the later stages of the revolt, while the peasants continued to sack monasteries and religious foundations, they spared in many cases the seats of the nobles, accepting them as natural allies. Small townships also opened their gates to the rebels, generally following a rising of the lower classes within the municipalities. It is to be noted, however, that though in these conquered towns the rebels were, for the time, in control, rarely was property abolished or a complete levelling carried out; the insurgent town elements had different aims from those of the peasants. As a consequence, when the tide turned against the rebels, the former authorities of the towns had only to emerge from their temporary retirement to assert themselves fully.

The chief danger to the rebels in South-west Germany were the forces of the Swabian League, which were being collected by its general, Georg von Truchsess. But while some military action was planned against these forces, the movement of revolt spread further to the north. Münzer travelled as its harbinger towards the regions he knew, where he had prepared the people for violent methods. Soon Thuringia was up in arms, and the Saxon Elector's watchman on the Wartburg could signal the oncoming of the rebel bands. Frederick the Wise was on his death-bed when he heard the news, and he said, with that wisdom that was characteristic of him: "The poor are oppressed in many ways by us secular and spiritual lords; if God so wills that the common man rule, so will it be." The news came that Erfurt had fallen and was a prey to the levellers. Luther took active measures. He gave his pastors earnest injunctions to go out among the rebel bands and convert them to the orthodox Lutheran doctrine, to turn them from violence, and persuade them to be satisfied. He himself passed through their bands. But they treated him summarily. He found that all the heresies of the sects flourished among them. They demanded that he should declare himself for their cause, their theology, and their social doctrine. When he refused and tried to urge his own doctrine, they would not listen and called him the slave of princes. The two social orders were in a blunt opposition, and no doctrinal compromise was possible. In a state of rage and fright, Luther regained the safety of Wittenberg. In the south, the army of the Swabian League was fighting successfully against the insurgents. In the north, Philip of Hesse was collecting his troops. Luther published his appeal to the armies of the established order.

Up to this time, and for some years still, Luther supported the principle that no prince was justified in rebelling against the imperial authority, not even on religious grounds. He would not even sanction armed defence against the Catholic Empire. In this the Elector Frederick had concurred, and had been so logical as not to take forcible action against religious sectarians like Münzer even when Luther implored him to do so. In one of his last letters, Frederick seemed to recommend this attitude with respect to the peasants' revolt, and wrote: " Even if the peasants get the upper hand now, God will punish them for it." Luther, however, considered the autocracy of the prince within his territory should be as absolute as that of the Emperor in his Empire; while the lower subjects have no right to revolt, the autocrat has the duty of protecting the established order. The most crass manifestation of this principle was the work Luther now wrote against the peasants. Its title is indicative of its contents—*Against the Murdering and Pillaging Bands of the Peasants.*[1] It is a raging, cruel appeal for the

[1] *Wider die räuberischen und mörderischen Rotten der Bauern*, 1525, Vol. XVIII.

extermination of the rebels. The overlords, Luther
says, must recognise in their hearts that they are
the cause of the disturbances; but then he recommends the matter to God, and summons the nobles
and princes to slay the peasants without mercy.
" Therefore strike, throttle, thrust, each man who
can, secretly or openly—and bear in mind that
there exists nothing more poisonous, more harmful,
more devilish, than a rebellious man. As one must
slaughter a mad dog. . . ." Besides that, all who
fall fighting for the cause of law and order are
called " true martyrs for God," and promised salvation as a consequence—a remarkable lapse on the
part of a theologian whose first tenet was the
inefficacy of good works in God's sight. To such
an extravagance could his dread of social upheaval
lead Luther.

The lords scarcely needed Luther's encouragement to carry out thorough reprisals on the peasants.
They cut the ill-organised, isolated detachments of
peasants to pieces in Swabia and Franconia, and
finally destroyed them at the bloody Battle of
Frankenhausen—bloody because of the slaughter of
the rebels, who were caught unawares and offered
little resistance. Aristocratic leaders of the peasants
like Götz von Berlichingen betrayed and quitted
their peasant troops. The peasant leaders themselves were killed, or tortured in imprisonment
before being executed. Münzer was captured and
met a sad end. The persecution of the rebels after
their defeat was equally pitiless, whole batches being

destroyed after giving themselves up. Chief in this bloodthirsty pursuit was Philip, the Landgrave of Hesse, soon to become a pillar of the Lutheran Church. There was no one to take the part of the peasants, and no longer any discussion of their rights. But many voices were raised against Luther. There was a common feeling that he was responsible in some measure for the rising—not only had he been at first looked on as their champion by the peasants, but also they had rejected ecclesiastical authority in the same way as he. Many humanists, as Erasmus and Pirckheimer, had earlier turned away from his reform because of the demagogy they feared lay hid within it. And of course the Catholic Church pressed this point in its polemic against the arch-heretic. But also in his own intimate circle Luther was censured. Rühel, Luther's brother-in-law, a town-councillor in Mansfeld, and a staunch adherent of Lutheranism, wrote to him: " I fear you wish to be a prophet to the overlords, that they bequeath to their progeny a waste land. For they punish to such a degree that I fear Thuringia and Mansfeld will take long to revive," and five days later he wrote again: " Many of those favourably disposed towards you are amazed that this pitiless throttling has been sanctioned the tyrants by you. . . . It is publicly said that you are afraid for your skin and are flattering Duke George by approving his actions. . . ." Thus the prudent councillor and his circle criticised Luther's attitude on economic as well as moral grounds. It is, how-

ever, incorrect to attribute Luther's action to
psychological motives; such an analysis would be
justified only if it had been in complete discord with
his formerly enunciated principles; and actually
this is not the case. He works quite consistently on
principles which are implicit in his religious doctrine.
He maintained the justice of his writing against the
peasants publicly and privately. He wrote in reply
to Rühel that one should have no remorse in punish-
ing the peasants; it was a pity to kill them, but
necessary. He adds: " If there are innocent men
among them, God will certainly preserve and keep
them, as he did with Lot and Jeremiah," a principle
which would justify any and every wrongdoing.
He published also the *Missive concerning the Harsh
Pamphlet against the Peasants*,[1] a defence of his former
work. In this he does not in the least admit that
he was in the wrong, but fulminates all the more
intolerantly against the remonstrances of his accusers.
" A rebel is not worthy of being answered with
reason," he cries, and cites the destruction of the
Amalekites by Saul—Luther too, then, found justification for violence in the Old Testament, like the
rebels. He distinguishes again between the secular
and religious sphere, and shows the different
principles ruling each, absolutism in the former and
" freedom " in the latter. God has shown the
peasants, he says, how things have hitherto gone
too well with them, and how in future they should
consider it a gracious privilege to keep one of two

[1] *Sendbrief von dem harten Büchlein wider die Bauern*, Vol. XVIII.

cows, and to give away the other as tax. " The
ass will have blows and the mob be ruled with
violence." After thus reaffirming his loyalty and
his opposition to all rebelliousness, Luther makes
concessions to humaneness. He says that pardon
should be meted out to such peasants as confess
their fault, and censures the lords for not having
pardoned the repentant. " Strike bravely in the
fight; but after the victory pardon all the remain-
ing." The conquered should be allowed to return
to their homes in peace. In his usual violent way,
Luther passionately imputes all the guilt for the
unnecessary slaughter of the defenceless peasants to
the lords, and does not accept any part of the
responsibility. Later, in the *Table Conversations*, he
once said: " I, Martin Luther, slaughtered in the
revolt all the peasants, for I commanded that they
should be slain; all their blood is on my head.
But I remit it to our Lord God, who commanded
me to speak so," thus finally renouncing responsibility for his passionate attack on the representatives
of a social reform his class could not tolerate.
Another reflection of his later years shows his lack
of sympathy towards the peasant class. " I rejoice,
that God has deprived the peasants of this great gift
and consolation, that they cannot hear music . . .":
music was, for Luther, the most precious gift of God
after theology. Such expressions of hatred for the
peasants, the masses, are common in Luther's works.

Luther declared himself against the order which
the peasants wished to impose on two grounds:

first, because the religion they wished to introduce was false; secondly, because they drew from their religion the sanction of their social reforms. In the preceding chapter of this book the idea of Lutheran orthodoxy was examined, and the reasons for Luther's opposition to the sects analysed. His authoritarianism on this point was seen to be the result of his class policy. The principle of the inviolability of the secular order can be seen to be also in harmony with Luther's class policy. But at this point we have not the right to say that this principle was erected by Luther merely to assure the interest of his class. For, just as he did not allow to the peasants the right of rebellion against their constitutional overlords, so he did not allow the prince, his supporter, the right of rebellion or of armed defence against the Emperor, his overlord. It seems as if this principle were a logical deduction from his theology, maintained irrespective of Luther's advantage. But the development of the times forced Luther to unfold what was implicit in these abstract formulations on which his reform was founded. An examination of Luther's theory of law and of the relations between the Emperor and the princes of the Empire will show a development in Luther's theory of secular authority which will once again reveal the basic principles of his reform.

(b) *Luther's Theory of Law*

It is evident that Luther did not meet the problems posed by the peasants' rebellion without theoretical preparation. Before he knew of the risings he had expounded his view of the true Christian attitude towards established authority.[1] The peasants were completely misled when they believed he would have an active sympathy with a demand for reforms, even though he thought the reforms good. His theory of law must now be examined.

It is of use to glance at the main lines of medieval legal theory, for Luther's thought here is no more "original" than his theology. For St. Thomas there was a direct connexion between earthly law and divine. Earthly law is based on certain innate ideas of right and justice instilled in our reason by God, so that our righteousness is a reflection of God's. The judgments of the law are therefore subject to the approval of our notion of justice; when the law and our conviction of right come into opposition it is necessary that the former should be modified in favour of the latter. Thus the powers of this world, whose representative the law is, have no absolute control over the individual, but are obeyed only subject to the approval of the conscience. Translated into philosophical terms, this was expressed thus by St. Thomas: the reason is the supreme governor; will is merely the executive power of the reason; "will has not the nature of law unless it itself is governed by reason." With this went naturally a tendency to believe in the goodness of man's nature and the freedom of the

---

[1] In *Wider die himmlischen Propheten* . . . *January* 1525; cf. pp. 112–113.

will. St. Thomas allowed to the earthly order a divine quality, but insisted that there were higher forces whose function it is to correct it.[1]

Another school of thought came into existence which challenged the very basis of St. Thomas' thought. For Duns Scotus and William of Occam the law was the direct expression of the will of God. Our notions of good and evil had no roots in innate ideas, but by a sudden decision God could, if He wished, completely reverse our system of right and wrong. There was no relation at all between divine and human righteousness. The value of the law was to be a constraint, a mortification for man, whose reason is not a reflection of the divine Reason. This system St. Thomas had dubbed "more an iniquity than a law"; it led to Gabriel Biel's formulation that law would exist "even if God did not exist." Its political bearing was, that while it refused to the secular order any divine element, it yet made this order inviolable, since its value was to be a constraint. It recognised no standards whereby the justice of the law could be judged, and raised the established order above the correction of the individual conscience. This theory of law was supported by a change in the conception of the ruler. While for St. Thomas the King was instituted by God to carry out His commands, and was liable to be punished if he took to evil ways, for later medieval writers the thesis was taken from Roman law that the King was elected by the people. But

[1] Cf. Lagarde, *Esprit politique de la Réforme*, pp. 18 ff.

this apparently democratic point of view served only authoritarian ends. For, assuming that the King has been elected by the people, there was no further means of correcting him. The people had to abide by its bargain. This theory, represented in its most extreme form by Marsilio of Padua, implied the breakdown of medieval society and the establishment of absolute principalities. Together with this doctrine went a sharp division between the spiritual and secular sphere and the scope of the spiritual and secular authorities, between Church and State. And it was bound up with the belief in the evilness of man's nature and the enslavement of man's will.

From the beginning Luther showed himself to be of the progeny of these thinkers, though he affirmed his descent fully only after being thrown into the battleground of his times. His desire to apply himself solely to devotional and theological study, his disinclination for and denial of the importance of political thought, marked him as an opponent of St. Thomas. Equally his scorn of the secular order, or rather of the spiritual value of secular office, expressed in so many works throughout his life, marks him as an Occamist.[1] The sharp distinction

---

[1] Cf. in *Sermon on Exodus xix and xx* (Sept. 10, 1525), Vol. XVI, pp. 404-5. " The kings of this world can only traffic in gold, silver, money, and goods, possess wealth and power, throttle and torment the people, tax, flay and skin their subjects . . . they cannot keep off sin, death, the devil, hell, sickness or misfortune. . . ." Cf., too, his scorn of the jurists, " who exalt the value of works."

he makes between the secular and spiritual sphere shows him also to be of this school.[1] But he himself reveals most clearly the underlying tendency of this distinction, which Troeltsch has defined generally as denoting the emancipation of the secular bodies from the control of the Church. For, after reiterating that he himself was a pure theologian and that the study of theology had nothing to do with human institutions, he was forced to take sides in the political struggles of the times, often to urge the political powers to action, and did not shirk justifying his conduct with texts from the Bible. And this was the result, not of a chance position he held, but of the doctrine he expounded. From the beginning, then, we can see the deeper meaning of the theoretical distinction between the secular and spiritual sphere; he himself sums it up in the *Commentary to the Romans*, written in 1515–16: "All established power whose orders have the force of law is instituted by God, and it is this power which gives effect to His commandments." [2]

There are various contradictions in Luther's statements concerning the nature of law. At one time he does not admit that any land can be well ruled by law alone, at another he describes with admiration the institutions of the heathen. But more subtle is the confusion in his theory of the relationship between the law of Moses and the

[1] Cf. *Von der Freiheit eines Christenmenschen.*
[2] *Commentarius in Epistolam ad Romanos*, ed. Ficker, Vol. I, p. 115.

established contemporary law. In an earlier chapter I showed this confusion to consist in his attributing divinity to the judgments of the Mosaic law, while equating this law with all established order.[1] Thus, all judgments according to established law are judgments of God. Laws cannot be called good or bad in themselves, but the system of law in any land is sacred. " The powers that be are ordained of God." Law is, from a formal point of view, divine, and no revolt against it is permissible.

By this doctrine Luther had answered those men who had attempted to carry through reforms based on the law of Moses. He had, however, to refute another aspect of their evangelicalism which presented a problem of an opposite nature. This was their claim that as Christians they were delivered from the law and had no need to obey ecclesiastical or secular commands.[2] It touched Luther closely, since this thesis of St. Paul's had been a battering-ram in his attack on the Papacy. He now expounded it in his own way. The freedom of a Christian, he said in the *Instruction of Visitors,* consists in this, " that Christ does not bind us to the ceremonies and constitution of Moses, but that Christians may use the legal code of all lands, the Saxons the Saxon law, others Roman law." This piece of sophistry is condemned out of Luther's own mouth, for if Christ came to deliver Jews from the law of Moses, and the law of

---

[1] Cf. Chap. IV, pp. 109 ff.
[2] Cf. the conflict with the Antinomians, who wished to avoid all mention of the Mosaic law in the pulpit.

Moses is in no way different in character from other
law, then the duty of the Christian of any time, if he
puts himself in the place of Christ, is to deliver himself and his fellow-men from the established law. In
other places Luther grants that the true meaning of
the delivery from the law is that men are saved by
faith, and not by works. But he never admits that
this means that men can ignore works or the law.
Not only is the law essential to man, since " by the
law is knowledge of sin " (Romans iii. 20)—Luther
says the law of Moses should be studied in order to
learn what sin is and what are the punishments of
God [1]—but also the true Christian will, after he has
attained the perfect faith, accomplish of his own
motion the works of the law. So closely are good
works and faith connected, that Luther emphasises
the necessity of teaching the people that worldly as
well as heavenly welfare will result from keeping
God's commandments.[2] He himself feels his position to be so insecurely founded that he writes: "And
it is not necessary that men should subtly dispute
whether God gives us merits for the sake of our works,
it is enough that one should teach that God rewards
and nourishes such as do these works, since He has
promised it, without merit of ours. . . . But many
cry: There is no merit in works. It would be much
better, if one urged the people to do good works and
let the sharp disputations fall. For it is true that
God gives us good things in order to fulfil His

---

[1] *Unterricht der Visitatoren*, Vol. XXVI, p. 203.
[2] *Ibid.*, p. 206.

promise to us, and not for the sake of our works;
but still good works, which have been commanded
by God, must be done." [1] Many papists might have
answered in similar terms to Luther's original
challenge. " Good works " in Luther's definition
are, however, good only in so far as they are the
fulfilment of a command. Where the confusion
arises is that, although Luther has equated Mosaic
and Saxon law, yet the keeping or contravening of
certain (not all) of the commands of the Mosaic law
is fraught with more dangers than is the case with
the Saxon law. In particular, the Ten Commandments have a peculiar sanctity, and their infringement brings a peculiar punishment from God; but
Luther explains this on the ground of their being the
most fundamental definition of the relationship between God and man, and man and man, and uni-
versally valid. They are not different in quality
from other laws, but more general.

But Luther does not stop at enjoining men to
accomplish good works. All Christians of the true
belief, he said, automatically accomplish good works.[2]
This means that they would be recognisable by their
observance of the commands of Moses. Anyone,
then, who neglected to observe the commands of
Moses proved himself thereby to be a bad Christian.
On this ground Luther could justify the re-introduc-
tion of ecclesiastical punishments. He advocated

[1] *Unterricht der Visitatoren,* Vol. XXVI, p. 206.
[2] As St. Paul says: " Love is the fulfilling of the Law,"
Rom. xiii. 10.

the use of the ban of excommunication for such crimes as blasphemy, repeated lying, adultery, gluttony.[1] More serious crimes, such as the teaching of false doctrine or of rebellion, should be reported at once to the representative of the lord of the land, and the delinquents handed over to the secular arm to punish. Thus for Luther, as for the medieval Church, the observance of certain exercises which the Church imposed was imperative, but such observance did not, in his view, bring with it any divine merit. He reintroduced the formal aspects of the medieval Catholic Church as a sort of pharisaism.

Luther's wish to reinstate the ecclesiastical ban is of great importance in showing that, if he had had the power, he would have gone further in the establishment of an ecclesiastical autocracy than he did, and would have approximated to the form of the Papacy against which he had so passionately striven. But actually his Church had very little power over men. It needed the executive power of the State. And eventually all questions of discipline, moral and theological, were referred to the State, to the ruler. This was the logical outcome of his first definition of the distinction between secular and spiritual activity. Like his main authority, St. Paul, he had said that the secular sword had been instituted by God to defend the faith and punish evil-doers. On purely spiritual matters the priests were to decide by reference to the Word of God. Since, however, the Word

[1] *Unterricht der Visitatoren*, p. 233.

of God proved ambiguous, or at any rate priests showed themselves unwilling to accept Luther's interpretation, his doctrine could only be established by force. Here the prince had to act; and in his judgment of spiritual matters, as of secular, he is, for Luther, "not a terror to good works, but to evil . . . he is the minister of God to thee for good" (Romans xiii. 1 and 2). In spite of the reiterated belief that the world is Satan's dwelling-place, that the law is qualitatively not divine, the notion that good is actually the aim of the law creeps continually into Luther's thought, and is used for polemical purposes. Thus, though he at times condemns the servants of the law, the jurists, in the strongest terms, saying that they exalt the merit of works and are servants of the devil, Luther repeatedly associates their calling with that of the priest. In his sermon *That Children should be kept to School*, 1530, he says that for a Christian State priests and jurists are necessary.[1] The preservation of the social order went hand in hand with the preservation of the Church. And Luther's theory of law was such that the absolutism of the ruler was affirmed on one side, and his Church's authority assured on the other through its being the devoted slave of the established order. The converse of this was that any revolt—the revolt of doctrine in the Church and the revolt of a body of subjects in the State—was opposed by Luther; and that his theory of law made both of the same nature and both an offence against the ordinance of God.

[1] *Predigt, man solle Kinder zur Schule halten*, Vol. XXX, p. ii.

Heresy and rebellion become in his eyes one concept, and the punishment of the ruler and of God identical. This was in effect a revival of Judaism, though the secular head was even more uncontrolled under Luther's system than under that of Moses.[1] Luther goes further, too, in that he modifies the very sayings of Christ to fit them into this system, as, for instance, when he says that " they that take the sword shall perish with the sword " is to be understood as " they that, of their own initiative and without the command of their ruler, take the sword, will be punished." [2] He could justifiably write of himself: " For such honour and glory has been given to me by God's grace . . . that since the times of the Apostles no doctor, nor writer, no theologian, nor jurist has *confirmed*, instructed, and solaced the conscience of the secular estates in so glorious and clear a fashion as I have done, by the especial grace of God. . . ." [3] In such a way was accomplished the revolution in the theory of law which had been developing since St. Thomas.

(c) *Luther and the Imperial Authority—his Conception of the State*

By the sharp division in his theory between secular and religious, between natural and divine law,

---

[1] In *Katechismuspredigt*, 1528, he applies Moses' command " Honour thy father " to the ruler: it is equivalent to " Avoid rebellion," and is an absolute, divine command. (Vol. **XXX**, p. 70.)

[2] *Unterricht der Visitatoren*, Vol. **XXVI**, p. 208.

[3] *Verantwortung*, Vol. **XXXVIII**, p. 103.

Luther did not imply that rationalism was to rule in the former sphere. He meant merely that different axioms were valid for the two spheres. The fundamental rule of natural law is that its subjects are ordered in a hierarchy, with a dominant head and subordinate members; and this was the order which Luther declared inviolate for the State. Machiavelli had proposed some such absolutism for certain concrete reasons, and had had more than an inkling of the expediential nature of governmental organisations. He wished the ruler to maintain his position and the people to tolerate it through a clear recognition of their own advantage. For Luther, on the other hand, the secular order, although working on its own natural principles, was instituted so by God. Its form and principles were sacred because God had made them. " Earthly government is a divine order and estate," as he repeats many times. Machiavelli's Prince, the product of an enlightened and clearsighted mind, was veiled by Luther in all the traditional wrappings of divinity. And the appointed task of government is, as he puts it most pregnantly in the sermon, *That Children should be kept to School*, 1530, to preserve property, and so to keep men above the level of beasts.[1]

At the commencement of his reformatory polemics, this theory caused no difficulties in Luther's plan of action. He looked to the Emperor Maximilian to be the natural leader in the purification of the Church, as he was the leader of the secular order. Indeed,

[1] Vol. XXX, ii, p. 555.

for the majority of the discontented parties in Germany the Emperor seemed their natural supporter. In the general mind he was the natural antithesis to the Pope. The burghers, the imperial knights, even the peasants, expected aid from him in their struggle against their enemies. Brant, Wimpheling, Hutten make idealised images of him. Only the princes of the Empire and the Pope knew that the Emperor had his own interests, which might, and often did, clash with theirs. Luther shared in this idealisation of the Emperor, this belief that the Emperor was the defender of the rights of the common man. Maximilian of course used the reformer as a pawn in his contest with the princes and the Pope, and at times seemed favourable, at times the ally of the Church. Luther did not lose hope in him, however, and on his death transferred his trust to his successor Charles V. Thus *To the Christian Nobility* of 1520 is addressed to the Emperor as to the princes and other authorities within the Empire.

This work, however, marks a change in Luther's attitude. It is the first time that he proposes a method of reform; and at the same time he grants to the princes and other minor lords and ruling bodies the possibility of taking the initiative, of acting without the sanction of the Emperor. As a result, a certain amount of secularisation of ecclesiastical property went on, though the lords showed themselves indifferent to the welfare of their subjects. The communities asserted themselves in some places and carried through the reform themselves, but often conflict ensued between those who took over the Church revenues and those who felt morally responsible for the souls of the people. The antagonism of interest, which the sectarians most clearly pointed out, between civic authorities and religious reformers, existed in some measure in all places. In 1523 Luther made a pronouncement of his views concerning the position of the princes in society, in a work called *On Secular Government, How Far Obedience is Due to it*.[1] The immediate occasion for this book was the persecution of Lutherans in Catholic countries, but Luther's statements apply to the general relationship of princes and subjects. The secular order, he says, has been founded by God in order to punish evil-doers and to protect the good. Worldly power has, however, not the task of making men good; this is the function of the Church. Nor are subjects justified in opposing the will of their lords. For instance, no prince is justified in demanding of Lutherans to give up their Lutheran books. If, however, wicked princes do so, the Lutherans should not comply with their demand until force is applied, when they are, even then, not justified in replying with force. Luther adds, " A clever prince is a *rara avis*, a pious one even more rare; they are mostly the greatest fools and the worst rascals on earth." He makes one exception. Christians must not bear the sword in their own interest, but they may do so in the interest

---

[1] *Von weltlicher Oberkeit.*, Vol. XI. It is to be noted that the Elector of Saxony was particularly pleased with this book, and had a manuscript copy made of it for his own private use.

of their neighbours; princes may do so also in the cause of their subjects, to protect the pious from the attacks of the wicked.[1] War is permissible to the princes in this cause, but only on one condition, that the princes are led by a clear intuition of the rightness of their action—"a special inspiration and faith." This work was written with an eye rather to the relations between unruly subjects and their lords than to those between the lords themselves. Its conclusion is that while nothing can justify armed action by the subjects, the princes may use force to coerce threatening elements; Luther thus shows confidence in the "inspiration" by which they will act. But while giving this right to the princes Luther does not allow them to fight against the Emperor— an eventuality not very probable at that moment. He writes: "No prince shall war against his over-lord, that is, his King and Emperor, or whoever be his liege-lord, but shall relinquish what is taken." This seems the same principle as Luther laid down for the subjects of princes, but it bears the contradiction that the princes are on the one side permitted to take up arms for their faith, and on the other are not allowed to fight against the Emperor.

It is not to be thought that Luther enunciated this doctrine in the belief that the princes would work for the cause of God. At first he had believed this, and

[1] Luther wrote: "In such a case one must risk life and property for one's neighbour. In such a war it is Christian, and a work of love, to throttle, rob, burn the enemy with a good courage," Vol. XI, p. 277.

had hoped the reform of morals and the Church would come from them. By 1523, however, he was growing disabused on this point. In his usual extravagant way he poured out his invective against the slackness and perversity of the princes and nobles. He called them " tyrannous and raging lords," " fools and rascals "; he told them openly that it was their misrule that was responsible for the miseries of the peasant rising; he cried, " In the courts there rule faithlessness, money-speculation, selfishness, avarice," etc. In 1524, seeing little fruit from his appeals to the nobles, he called on the town-councillors to carry out the most necessary reforms, such as the institution of schools. Their wickedness was so profound and their lethargy in his cause so immovable that he confidently expected the only solution—the Day of Judgment. In spite of this, he was the ardent supporter of the system which depended on them, and for the sake of their authority opposed the sectarians who wished to usher in Christ's kingdom. Only under their ægis were the values he most esteemed secure.

The first test of Luther's principle of the inviolability of the imperial authority came after 1525. By the victory of Pavia, Charles was all-powerful in a pacified Europe. At the Diet which was held in 1525 he promised summary punishment to all of his subjects who supported the Lutheran heresy, but put off the decision as to ways and means till the next year, hoping that some of the Lutheran princes would in the meanwhile be won over to the more mighty cause. John of Saxony, the successor of Frederick the Wise, and Philip of Hesse, who had turned to the Lutheran faith shortly before, used the breathing space thus granted them to effect with others of their belief the League of Torgau, which bound its members to render mutual assistance in the event of an attack from the ecclesiastical party, and to prevent, if possible, the execution of the decisions of the Diet of Worms. Luther's sanction was asked, as the participation of all Lutherans was needed. He was sorely put to it to justify a league formed in defence of his religion which disrupted the Empire and the imperial authority, and for a time he condemned it. Its formation was urgent, however, and in the end he admitted that a league formed to meet a specific eventuality was permissible, in order to scare the godless, but that no league was right and proper that was directed against the ruling power. This was hedging, he knew, though the political situation demanded it; but he salved his conscience in a little work he published at the time, in which he said that no violence is permissible against a ruler, even though he break all solemn oaths and promises given to his people. It seems that, while he still insisted that his principle stood firm—and in the face of his recent judgments concerning the peasants he had to reiterate this—he made an inward reservation to suit the particular case.[1] He was not likely to be able to justify this in his theology, for he

[1] Cf. also the inward reservation he made with respect to Philip of Hesse's bigamy.

had fulminated in particular against the Catholic doctrine of reserved cases. His doctrine did not betray him at this time, for the apprehensions of the Lutherans did not materialise, as the League of Cognac between the Papacy and France unbalanced Charles V's power and security, and no advance was made on the Lutherans.

In 1528 relations between the Catholic and Lutheran princes again became strained, and the former again threatened action against the adherents of the banned religion. Although still unwilling to sanction war, Luther did so this time with a good conscience, for the Emperor was not engaged and the initiative lay with the Catholic princes acting upon their own responsibility. Thus, by arming in defence, the Lutherans were not combining against their overlord. The danger was again averted by the external situation, but this recurrent mobilisation made bad blood between the adversaries, and both were thereby prepared for a future bloody and obstinate struggle. As the Diet of Augsburg of 1530 grew near, at which Charles, freed from his many wars, promised to deal finally with the heretic princes, the Protestants knew that they must make ready for the worst. They made strenuous efforts to summon up all their military resources and allies. In particular, the princes attempted to make an alliance with Zwingli. Zwinglianism was already rife in the south of Germany and Switzerland. It had conquered big cities there, and had, as a consequence, the form of a republic. From the locality in which it spread it inherited a traditional antagonism towards the Empire, and opposition to the imperial authority was a tenet which followed naturally from its political form. Like Luther, Zwingli had repressed with great severity the activities of the enthusiasts and levellers; but differently from the subject of the Elector of Saxony, he was ready to take violent measures against the imperial oppressor. Philip of Hesse pressed therefore for an alliance with this strong body in the south. But a main difficulty existed. Zwingli had accepted Carlstadt's interpretation of the sacrament of the Communion, that the bread and wine are but symbols of God's presence—it was in accordance with the partially democratic nature of his Church that he could be more rationalistic than the absolutist Luther. And this interpretation was for Luther an abominable heresy and a sign of godlessness. As incapable of fusion as are the principles of absolutism and democracy, so incapable of fusion were the eucharistic doctrines of Luther and Zwingli. Philip of Hesse brought all his powers and energy into play to bring Luther to sanction this heresy. Bucer, the most subtle go-between of the times, as his later activity in England was to show, used all his skill on Luther. But Luther, though occasionally wavering because of the immediate benefits the alliance would bring, refused in the end any compromise with the Zwinglians. Many of his own followers in theology, his closest disciples, were bitterly disappointed; but what is astonishing is the severe logic with which

Luther adhered to the theological, as to the political principle, of his reformation.

Seeing that the alliance with the Zwinglians was impossible of achievement, the Lutherans set about strengthening their own league and preparing for the attack they confidently expected. And knowing Luther's scruples, the jurists of the princes sought a legal justification for a league against the imperial authority. They could at first come to no better decision than that armed resistance against the Emperor was permissible, since it was a principle of law that those wrongfully oppressed may defend themselves. This principle Luther had declared false shortly before. If accepted, it meant that the risings of the peasants had been just, and should not have been condemned by jurists or theologians. Also it meant the recommencement of the old anarchy in Germany; it was merely a new formulation of the old right of feud (*Fehderecht*), which had allowed anyone feeling himself unjustly condemned to seek his rights by force of arms. During the Diet of 1530, when this decision was come to, Luther could not be at Augsburg, being under the ban of the Empire, but stayed in safety at Coburg, near enough to Augsburg to supervise Melanchthon's actions and declarations. As a consequence, the jurists applied to Bugenhagen, Luther's trusted friend, the pastor at Wittenberg, for his opinion. Bugenhagen agreed with the jurists' ruling, saying that in matters of religion the Emperor had no right of jurisdiction, and justifying armed resistance to the Emperor by examples from the Old Testament, the happy hunting-ground for the consciences of all friends of violence. This was a complete reversal of Luther's position; it is interesting as foreshadowing the later abjectly submissive attitude of Lutheranism towards the State. Luther, however, called on for his opinion, again maintained his former statements. He told the Elector that it was not necessary for him to protect his own or anyone else's interests against the Emperor. He recommended that the Elector should lay his complaints before the Diet and openly state his reasons for not having complied with the orders given at the Diet of Worms, claiming at the same time a council of the Church to judge of Luther's heresy. In another letter Luther said that even if the Emperor used violence, no campaign should be entered on against him. God would find means to save his elect and make peace. In a considered " Opinion " he sent to the Elector he reasserted this point of view, stating that the authority of the Emperor could be disregarded only if the Empire and princes unanimously deposed him. Meanwhile, Zwingli was pressing for a general offensive alliance among all Protestants and advocating a league with the Venetian Republic and the French, political enemies of Charles.

It seems certain that Luther even at this point believed it possible that the Emperor could be won over to his cause.[1] Though he was a very keen

[1] Even after the Diet had broken up, he wrote: " The Emperor Charles is an excellent man; he hopes to make peace

observer of happenings that went on before his eyes he was always ignorant of diplomatical actuality. But after the Recess of Augsburg, when the Protestant doctrine, as formulated by Melanchthon in the Confession of Augsburg, had finally been condemned by the Emperor, no doubts could linger in Luther's mind. On the first rumours of the decisions of the Recess, Luther still refused to believe. In the *Gloss on the Supposed Edict of the Emperor*,[1] Luther cried that his doctrine had not been understood and that the Emperor had been tricked by his underlings, Luther's enemies. On the latter he pours out his invective. He calls them traitors and evil-doers, mad beasts and obscene swine—" whether they be princes or bishops, who carry out their desperate, evil designs in the name of the Emperor." But Luther was already prepared for the final step. Although the Elector of Saxony expressed himself in favour of Luther's view, it was clear to all the politicians that the Emperor was to be identified with the papal cause. And the jurists, aware of Luther's grounds for opposing action against the highest authority of the Empire, set to work with great determination to overcome his scruples. They found the argument: the Emperor had acted beyond his powers in condemning the Lutheran doctrines. In matters of faith he was only the executive power of the Church.

---

and unity; I only do not know if he can do so, since he is encircled by so many devilish monsters." There was a deep tradition amongst all radical reformers that their reforms would be carried out by the head of the Empire.

[1] *Glosse auf das vermeinte kaiserliche Edikt*, 1531, Vol. **XXX**, iii.

It was necessary that an ecumenical council should first pronounce Luther's doctrine false before action could be taken against the heretics.[1] Since therefore the Emperor had acted *ultra vires*, it was permissible to those falsely judged to have recourse to illegal means of opposition. This formal protest was based on statements of old jurists, in particular of teachers of that canon law which Luther had claimed to have abolished. In this law it had been permissible to refuse to accept findings of judges who acted out of their competence. But this law was of a totally different nature from the law of the secular body. The Emperor, being the supreme juridical authority, could not transgress his powers; he was the supreme court of appeal. In spite of this, Luther gave way. He accepted the claim of the jurists that the competence of the Emperor to make this judgment was a matter for the jurists to decide. He allowed the princes to be their own judges.

For a little while Luther took up the position that these matters belonged to the sphere of the jurists, and that a simple theologian must busy himself with other affairs; and still he expressed his doubts about the rightness of opposition, and the legality of the league of Schmalkalden which had been formed by the Protestant Powers in 1530—"because the Gospel does not preach against earthly rights."

[1] Actually the Recess had proclaimed that a council of the Church should be convoked as soon as possible. And Luther, a little later, said that no council, not even an angel from heaven, could persuade him that he was wrong!

But he soon took up a more militant and positive attitude. Before 1531 was out he justified his change of principle. A prince *qua* prince is not a Christian, he declared, but had merely to defend his people, both their earthly and their spiritual welfare. In a virulent work directed against the Catholic Duke of Saxony, the cousin of his own lord, he stated, after comparing the Protestants to Abel and the papists to Cain: " When Emperor and ruler wage war against God and right, then shall no man pay obedience to them "; [1] and in his *Warning to his dear Germans*: [2] " If the papists were to dare a war, it might well be that God would awaken another Judas Maccabaeus. . . . Whoever then puts himself on his guard is not to be called rebellious. . . . Resistance against the bloodhounds should rather be called legitimate self-defence." In his customary whole-hearted way, Luther showered his invective on the papists, even on the Emperor, now that he felt himself justified in resisting them: he called for the most extreme and pitiless measures, once any opposition was necessary. And his theory developed similarly, so that soon he proclaimed it to be the sacred duty of the secular arm to fight in the cause of religion. We have seen, in the preceding chapter, how he gave the princes and lords all power over the religion of their subjects; [3] now he made it their duty to defend themselves against outward

[1] *Wider den Meuchler zu Dresden*, 1531, Vol. XXX, iii.
[2] *Warnung an seine lieben Deutschen*, 1531, Vol. XXX, iii.
[3] Cf. *Visitation Instruction* of 1527, Vol. XXVI, p. 81.

enemies.[1] He could say with Melanchthon: " For one must straightway take to arms, not only by worldly right, *but impelled by conscience.*" This attitude of Luther's presents a glaring contradiction to that he had held up till then. Within a few months he had swung round from reverence of the imperial authority to repudiation and scorn of it. His opponents had easy game with him, and Cochlaeus, a theological adversary of Luther's, had only to reprint the " Opinion " Luther had sent to his master in 1530 to show up his betrayal of his first principles. This work was again reprinted at the time of the later wars of religion, 1546–7, to the detriment of the Lutheran cause. But it was not on a doctrinal issue that the Lutheran cause could be crushed.

Meanwhile troubles inside and outside the Empire again made vain the projected action against the Lutherans. The Turks again were advancing into the Habsburg dominions. Charles also was making great efforts to secure the election of his brother Ferdinand of Austria as King of the Romans, so that his kinsman could represent him in the Empire during his enforced absences. Ludwig of Bavaria, an ardent Catholic, resented this strengthening of the Habsburg dynasty, and pressed the Protestants

[1] In *Table-Talk* (1539) he said that it was the duty of the electors and other princes of the Empire to resist the Emperor if he did anything against God and Right, and simplified difficulties of definition by saying that if the Emperor attacked any German land he did it in the cause of the Pope, the " godless arch-fiend " (*Tischreden*, Vol. IV, p. 240).

to unite with him to make this election a cause of civil war. This the Protestants refused to do, as they did not consider their position strong enough nor the occasion sufficiently important. Also, they had seen a sad example of military failure in South Germany, where Zwingli had been defeated and killed after rising against his Emperor. They contented themselves with binding themselves more firmly in the Schmalkaldic League. In 1532 the political situation was so serious for Charles that he made with the Protestant Powers a Religious Peace at Nürnberg. Here it was decided to suspend all questions of faith, including the restoration of ecclesiastical property, till after the sessions of a council of the Church, which was to be called within a short time. The *status quo* was guaranteed till the Church should have made its decision. All princes pledged themselves, however, to suppress in their dominions any disturbances which might arise on religious grounds—a general union of the princes against the common people. In return for these privileges the princes and authorities promised obedience to the Emperor and due help in his pending war with the Turks. This treaty, a continuation of that made between Charles and his restive subjects in 1526, was of incalculable value to the Protestant cause, endorsing the existence of a body within the empire which was hostile to the old idea of the Empire, and legalising by inference the conception of the independence of the principalities. It gave a great impetus to the process of Lutheranisation.

Luther's political doctrine was now fixed. There is no need, from the point of view of this book, to follow the history of the Protestant principalities and cities any further. The demands of the princes had overcome theological difficulties. There remained only the process of complete subservience of the Protestant religion to the State, which advanced now with great rapidity, as it was not complicated by doubts as to which political authority was on the side of Luther. The final decision of the theologians which we need to consider is the "Advice" drawn up by the leaders, Luther, Justus Jonas, Bucer, and Melanchthon, in which it is stated that armed resistance against religious opponents is a sacred duty of the secular lords; similarly, that it is a divine truth that they express, to support which they quote the Old Testament, with its many commands to the chosen people to exterminate nations of a different faith. They also sanction armed aggression on the part of the Protestants as soon as the imperial ban be issued against any member of the Schmalkaldic League. Luther could indeed legitimately boast of himself that "since the time of the Apostles the secular sword and rule has never been so clearly defined or so highly praised " as by him.[1]

The political order which corresponded to Lutheranism was then the absolutism of the principalities. Luther did not merely accept this reluctantly, but

[1] Cf. also *Vom Kriege wider die Türken*, Vol. XXX, ii, pp. 108 ff.

bolstered it up with all the means in his power. In spite of an apparently uneven development of his thought in this direction—and Lutheran historians often use phrases like " he did not realise," " he failed to see," etc.[1]—it was implicit in his attitude from the beginning. This can be seen most clearly from the " Great Catechism " of the Lutheran Church. It is apparent here that the family forms in the Lutheran ethic the basis for Luther's conception of the State. The prince is the " father of the land." All children who repeat this catechism are enjoined to honour their parents, and are told that to honour is more imperative than to love (. . . *Est enim honor res amore multis modis sublimior*). The prime virtues are " modesty, humility, reverence." And this attitude of subordination towards parents is applied in identically the same form to the prince and the political order. The key-note of the Lutheran ethic is humble thankfulness to God, shared by all classes, the rich man in his castle and the poor man at his gate. Christian love is subordinate to the reverence for the order of society. The authorities are loved for their care of the lower classes, and love their subjects with the wise but sometimes inscrutable love of parents. It is evidently the attitude of extreme Conservatism; and even Lutherans admit that the spread of Lutheranism among the lower classes has always been hindered more on political grounds than on dogmatic.[2] It

[1] Heinrich Boehmer, *Luther in the Light of Modern Research*, Chap. VI.
[2] Cf. Troeltsch, *op. cit.*, pp. 552 ff.

has been a powerful instrument in the hands of the authorities to crush all civil strife, particularly that based on the class struggle. Bismarck's oppression of the Social Democrats was the logical continuation of Luther's oppression of the peasants.

But it is not sufficient to define Luther as the servant of princes. In order to crush the various subversive theories of State, he had made use of his doctrine of the sacredness of the social order completely in their interest. But for long he was not satisfied with them, and expressed openly his distrust and condemnation of their policy. For long he insisted that they were subordinate to the Emperor. Only when the latter showed finally that he was opposed to Lutheranism did Luther see that there was no alternative, and cast himself fully into the arms of the princes. That he was able to effect such a *volte-face* without being stricken in his conscience shows that he did not feel that he was betraying a principle which he felt to be fundamental. His support of the princes can indeed be described as his tactics in the realisation of the interests that were truly his. Here the conclusions of Chapter IV again apply. Troeltsch calls Luther's ethic that of the agrarian, petty bourgeois class. The interests of the class of petty bourgeois he never betrayed. It would have been to the advantage of this class if an authority had existed above that of the princes. Since, however, Charles declared himself for the papists against the Lutheran princes, the choice for Luther was obvious. And having made this choice, there was no reason for him to shirk the most complete affirmation of the prince's absolutism. The preservation of this class, which was assailed from several sides, which was already showing itself to be economically threatened, needed the assertion that to each class, to prince, burgher, peasant, there belonged a peculiar task in society; and to preserve this division of classes, which was to last in Germany till the reforms of Stein ushered in, in 1808, the industrial period, the power of the absolutist prince was essential. Thus, though the history of Luther's development is the history of a compromise between the petty bourgeoisie (as it was defined in Chapter I) and the princes, he never wavered in his loyalty to his class, and, in general, defined the conditions of its existence.

CHAPTER VI

LUTHER'S ECONOMIC SYSTEM

IT has been shown that Luther in his religious and political thought supported absolutism. And it has been claimed that he did so because only under an absolutist system could the interests of his class be safeguarded. The reasons for this deduction were, shortly put: (1) He first supported a democracy in religious affairs, until events taught him that not all people would make the same deductions from Holy Scripture as he did; (2) he hoped to keep a check on the princes by declaring the Emperor's authority supreme; (3) after a little time he set his hope of an inward reform in the settled responsible middle class, giving up hope of a moral reform emanating from the princes, and continually railing at the way of life of the latter. He supported the princes because they would maintain the existing order, and this support was implicit in the very contradictions of his doctrine. It is, however, necessary to find a clear proof of this analysis that Luther was absolutist, not because he was a courtier, but because the needs of his class made it imperative, that he was primarily and fundamentally the representative of the petty bourgeoisie. This we shall find in his attitude to the economic problems of the times, that is to say, when he formulates his position with regard to the basic structure of society.

The period in which Luther lived is that in which a new economic principle asserted itself openly in Germany. This principle was that of usury, which was condemned by canon law, but which, partly through the Church's agency, had come to be accepted first in Italy and then in Europe generally. Through the practice of transforming ecclesiastical taxes into money payments, accumulations of money were created; and these were put in the hands of financial houses. From this store of cash, loans and advances could be made, and it soon became the custom to take interest on such loans. Money accumulated also through the extensive colonial exploitation carried on in the Mediterranean littoral by the Italian cities, but it is noticeable that the wealth and power of houses such as the Medici, who were practically only bankers, far exceeded those of the merchant-princes of Venice or Genoa. Usury had hitherto been mainly in the hands of Jews, as they were outside the prohibitions of canon law. But usury could now be carried on on such a large scale, that the interested parties could afford to ignore the Church's statement that money is in itself unproductive and by its nature incapable of bearing fruits. And there are evidences that canon law was modifying itself to embrace the new conditions created by the presence of money in large quantities.[1]

A further characteristic of these times is the

[1] Cf. Sir William Ashley, *Economic History.*

increase in monopolistic trading. The development of Antwerp from a place of periodical fairs to a permanent clearing-house made it all the more easy for rings of merchants to be formed, both for buying and for selling; and from this centre they could exercise considerable control over the inland producers and markets. The great banking houses and the monopolistic merchants were closely allied, though as the former developed they took the leading part. In the case of the most efficient of them their trade was definitely only the preparation and substructure of their financial business, or merely a by-product of it. The Fugger laid the foundation of their huge capital through the acquisition of silver-mines in the Tirol; being presented at the same time with copper-mines, they proceeded to control the copper market of Europe, this being, however, incidental to their main business. Many complaints were made in these times concerning the neglect of trading in favour of speculation, which was more lucrative, a classical example being Guicciardini's—" Formerly the nobles, if they had ready money, were wont to invest it in real estate, which gave employment to many persons and provided the country with necessities. The merchants employed capital of this kind in their regular trade, whereby they adjusted want and superfluity between the various countries, gave employment to many, and increased the revenue of princes and states. Nowadays, on the other hand, a part of the nobles and merchants (the former secretly through the agency of others, and the latter openly in order to avoid the risk and trouble of a regular profession) employ all their available capital in dealing in money, the large and sure profits of which are a great bait. Hence the soil remains untilled, trade in commodities is neglected, there is often increase in prices, the poor are fleeced by the rich, and finally even the rich go bankrupt." [1]

The class of bankers and monopolist merchants defined itself fairly clearly from the other strata of society in the sixteenth century. Luther was called on to express his opinion towards it, and could do so with all the more confidence since its principles seemed new and opposed to the common practice. As he says: " Taking of interest is injurious and harmful for many reasons: and in the first place, it is a new cunningly invented thing of these later dangerous times when no good things are invented and the minds of all men are set only on goods, honours, and pleasures." In many places in his early sermons he inveighs, like any other moralist of the times, against the greed and covetousness of man; [2] but the first clear exposition of his doctrine concerning interest-taking is to be found in the *Great Sermon on Usury*, 1520.[3]

---

[1] Quoted by R. Ehrenberg, *Zeitalter der Fugger* (Eng. translation, *Capital and Finance in the Age of the Renaissance*, p. 243). Guicciardini does not add that it was the political rivalry of the princes which was a chief incentive to the banking business. Without the continued wars and the consequent need for money there would have been a different development.

[2] Cf. *To the Christian Nobility*.

[3] *Grosser Sermon von dem Wucher*, Vol. VI.

Luther here asserts that the principles of Christ should govern trade—" Give to him that asketh thee, and from him that would borrow of thee, turn thou not away." Christ bids us, he says, to give without expectancy of gain, and especially to our enemies and those from whom we can hope for no return. What is right according to the law is not right in conscience; lending money or goods on interest is against the commands of Holy Scripture. After this general introduction, Luther turns to a more particular examination of interest-bearing loans. The trade in money is different from any other sort of trade; for in other trade there is gain to both sides, equally, but in a loan there is gain preponderantly to the creditor, who seeks only his own advantage. Usury is wrong because all the risk falls on the borrower, the creditor makes his profit without danger, without incurring the usual risks due to sickness, misfortune, etc. Luther attacks the reckless way in which land was mortgaged. It was the custom for improvident land-holders to raise mortgages without consideration for the value of their land or the possibility of paying off their debt, and in this way the usurers were ejecting the hereditary nobles.[1] Luther says that the value of

[1] From his peasant's point of view expropriation of landed property was a disaster. In *Unterrichtung wie sich die Christen in Mosen sollen schicken* he proposes a remedy which would have crippled mortgage—" It is also laid down in Moses that none should sell his property for an everlasting inheritance, but only for a year, and when the year was past, he would come again to the field or property which he had sold." This Mosaic law Luther says should be applied in Germany (Vol. XVI, p. 377).

different parts of estates should be estimated and mortgages raised on this value, not blindly on the security of the whole. Interest should be restricted. Above all, Luther insists that interest shall be understood in its original sense, that the creditor shall thereby take a share in the good or bad fortune of the debtor. The debtor shall be able to say to his creditor: " This year nothing is due to you; for I sold you my labour and pains at interest on the security of this and that property; but it has fallen out badly, the loss is yours and not mine. For if you have an interest in my gain, you must also have an interest in my loss, as is the nature of every purchase." In this Luther was returning to the most primitive Christian theory. He himself realises that this system was Utopian, and in the end says that, though lending without interest is the only right thing, yet, failing that, one should lend at a very low rate. It is evident that Luther deals in this work chiefly with mortgage, through which a considerable displacement in society was proceeding. His attitude cannot be said to be determined by consideration for the resultant impoverishment of society, for this was not a necessary consequence, but for the resultant impoverishment of a class whose existence he felt to be valuable.

In 1524, in a work entitled *On Commerce and Usury*,[1] Luther extended his criticism to the trading methods adopted by the big merchants. The date of this work is important, as it falls in a time when Luther

[1] *Von Kaufshandlung und Wucher*, Vol. XV.

has definitely thrown in his lot with the territorial princes and is helping to build up the new form of society, while the former work belongs to the period when he was mainly intent on criticising the old form. Thus there are concrete proposals for a method of reform in the later work which were missing in the earlier. As in *To the Christian Nobility* he prefaces his criticism with laments concerning the influx of luxuries from the East, spices, silks, etc., which he considers lead not only to immorality, to voluptuousness, pride, envy, but also to the impoverishment of the common people—this actually resulted, however, only when people occupying unproductive positions, such as nobles and princes, improved their standard of living at the expense of their subjects. These luxuries, he says, should be forbidden—" if we had a government and princes " —and he recommends the example of the patriarchs, who satisfied themselves with the barest necessities, cattle, wool, butter, etc., which they gained by the labour of their own hands. An agrarian community was his ideal. But, accepting the general form of society in which he found himself, he goes on to criticise some of its characteristics. The prices of commodities, he complains, are not calculated according to the labour expended in production and the needs of the producers, but according to the needs of the consumers, according to the scarcity; thus the middlemen, the merchants, make easy profits. He repeats the Christian admonishment that men should give out of love, but abandons hope of men's acting in a Christian way: " The secular sword must be red and sanguinary, for the world will and must be evil." He goes on to give a vivid description of the methods of chicanery employed by the big merchants and rings of merchants at the time. Some tempt their customers by offers of deferred payment, by which they gain a bigger price. Some, knowing they are the sole owners of a particular ware, sell as dearly as may be. Some buy up the whole market, effect monopolies, make rings to stabilise this state of affairs, and thus sell at their own price; where the princes and the town-councils make no provision against these methods, the common man is at the mercy of the monopolists. Some, seeing brother merchants in financial difficulties, take advantage of their opportunity to buy up their stock cheaply. Some, after they know they are bankrupt, still make loans, and then fly to a monastery; on promising to pay a low percentage of their debts, they are allowed back into business, and have made a thousand or two on the transaction; or they can buy from the imperial Court for one or two hundred gulden a moratorium for five years (*quinquennale*), which protects them for that time from their creditors —this was a particularly flagrant method of trickery, connived at by the imperial Court. Luther describes other sharp-practice habits common to the merchants, such as under-cutting and so on; he censures the dishonesty which brings them to such tricks as damping wool, silks, etc., in order to make them weigh more heavily. His hostility is most marked when he talks of the " Societies," the rings of merchants generally formed for a particular end, but having for the common man a seemingly permanent nature. Everyone, he feels, is dependent on them; they are insatiably avaricious, and never run the risk of losing—" For so it comes that in the whole world one must buy spices at the price they fix; they arrange the exchange. This year they put up the price of ginger, in a year's time that of saffron . . . if the ginger spoils or grows cheaper, they make it up on saffron." Above all, Luther condemns the investments placed by private individuals in commercial enterprises—" pure and simple usury."

Luther shows a very considerable knowledge of the ways of the powerful merchants of his times. He censures them on two points. First, they act in an unChristian way in tricking each other and their customers; secondly, they distort the natural law that every product has a proper price equivalent to the amount of work put into its production. Both these principles were disregarded by the economic system of the time. What were Luther's remedies? As for the first, he gives up any attempt at solving the contradiction between Christian doctrine and the contemporary methods of trade—" For it is lost labour to give counsel and instruction as to how one may deal in this matter in a Christian way and safely keep a pure conscience." He gives a sideblow at the merchants, saying that they would show a real Christian spirit if they ceased complaining about the oppression and robbery they suffered at the hands of the robber-knights, and accepted this as a judgment of God; Ulrich von Hutten had similarly justified the cutpurse tactics of his confederates. The only remedy to the ills of the system Luther found in the control of price, and again he had recourse to the kings, princes, and town-councils. Princes and kings, he says, must control the manipulations of the market. They must consider it their prime duty to look after the welfare of the common man, who otherwise will be fleeced by the merchants and will not be able to pay his taxes. But, Luther sadly recognises, the princes have themselves a finger in the merchants' pie. They also speculate and invest. Not merely the kings who possessed colonies, such as the kings of Portugal and Spain, were guilty of the same tricks as the merchants, but everywhere they were hand in glove with the merchants. Luther says, they hang petty thieves and consort with great ones. The town-councils also were infected with the same disease, but could provide a control such as Luther wished. He took no heed of the fact that with regard to the lower classes in the towns and the peasantry the town-councils, which were composed of the patriciate and the guilds, pursued the same policy of monopoly and oppression as the merchants. In spite of this, Luther could find no better solution than the control of commerce and price by the secular authorities, and he ends this work with an appeal to the secular powers to put matters right. The *Sermon on Usury* was printed with this writing

On Commerce and Usury, so Luther did not again broach the question of money-dealing pure and simple. He decides, however, that the only proper tax is an income-tax levied equally on all men. The tithe is, he says, the perfect tax, both according to divine and to natural law.[1] And in a good year the prince may levy as much as a fifth from his subjects.

Matters went their course in spite of Luther, and money speculation became more rife during the years following this writing. Investment became a common habit, and Luther himself, when entrusted with 500 gulden as an endowment for poor scholars at Wittenberg, had no scruples against asking how best he could lay it out at interest. Still, theoretically he did not change, and his last pronouncements are similar to his first. In a work of 1540 *To the Parish Priests that they shall Preach against Usury*,[2] he complains about the increase of usury, and says that those who take more than 5 per cent. are damned unless they repent. He gives his priests instructions that they shall refuse absolution to usurers who take high interest.[3] He repeats the medieval principle—" Money is an unfruitful thing, which I may not properly sell "; but he admits that only the Day

[1] Cf. *Unterrichtung wie sich die Christen in Mosen schicken sollen*, Vol. XVI, p. 376.

[2] *An die Pfarrherrn, wider den Wucher zu predigen*, 1540, Vol. LI.

[3] In the years previous to this date he had conducted a campaign against a noble who notoriously lent money at 30 per cent.: he hoped to institute an ecclesiastical ban against such persons.

of Judgment will put an end to this wicked custom. With regard to debts contracted under usurious conditions, he says, with his usual respect for the established order, that they must be paid. Other enemies of the new custom of dealing in money, such as Münzer, had said that even payment of such debts was a sin. Thus Luther, while opposing with all the might of his prestige the big monopolists and the extortionate money-lenders, did not agitate for a change of society, a change in the economic system, but advocated merely a control of this system. The modifications he urged or sanctioned—the control of production by the patriciate of the towns with the resultant local monopoly, and the restriction of interest to 5 per cent.—were those which favoured directly the stratum of society which he represented in every sphere, the petty, settled middle class. A certain degree of monopoly, a certain amount of money-dealing was necessary to this class; but in order to secure it against the enemies above it and below, the big merchants, and the increasing number of journeymen, control was necessary. And this control came, as always, from the princes, with whom they had common interests. Here the German princes differed essentially from the much more powerful kings of France, Spain, and England. These were wealthy and strong enough to control the big bankers and monopolists, and to use them for their own ends. The German princes, on the other hand, were at the mercy of this new class, and though able at times to flirt with them, were fundamentally their enemies.

The League of Schmalkalden, for instance, found great difficulty in raising a loan from the bankers, although many of the latter called themselves Protestant. Luther was clear-sighted enough to condone the errors of the German princes, their transient alliances with the bankers, and to rely on them to support his class against the foreign monopolists.

Luther took refuge, then, with the princes because the interests of his class demanded it. On what principle, however, did he justify the economic system of his class? In several works he recommends men to turn again to the patriarchal agrarian society to which biblical legislation applied. He talks of the " proper price " of articles as distinct from the market price. Henri Hauser talks of his " peasant and conventual prejudices." [1] But while these biblical conceptions still hover before his mind, Luther never takes any steps to define them clearly or to further their realisation. The vividness of his descriptions of the dealings of the monopolistic merchants and the extortionate usurers shows that he was well acquainted with the business methods of the day and well able to analyse them. But he does not turn his critical mind against the practices of his own associates, the good burghers of the towns. Here he satisfies himself with those general exhortations to leave evil and turn to good which have been the refuge of all those moralists who, not desiring change and yet being restive concerning the propriety of certain customs, thus salve their conscience.

[1] H. Hauser, *op. cit.*, p. 51.

His true attitude to these ideals of his can be seen in his behaviour towards the men who really wished to reform society on Christian principles. He turned with abhorrence from the idea of the communisation of property, and called the peasants and their leaders who pressed for this reform godless. And he did this not simply because he condemned the use of force, but because he believed in the sacredness of private property. Only through the preservation of private property, he said in 1530, is man kept above the level of the beasts. Thus he abandoned Christian principle, and accepted the basis of capitalistic society. His economic policy, it is true, is mixed up with biblical reminiscences which make it appear confused and idealistic when compared with that of Calvin; but it represents quite consistently the interests of a class large enough to safeguard itself for centuries against fresh developments, even though these were implicit in its principles.

CHAPTER VII

LUTHER AND THE CULTURE OF HIS TIMES

THIS book has so far discussed mainly the formal aspects of Luther's thought; owing to his relegation of spiritual values to the utmost privacy of the individual soul, his reforms of institutions and the like were bound to present mainly a purely formal appearance. These reforms I have defined as being those corresponding to the interests of the petty bourgeoisie, and this is particularly clear in the case of his proposed economic system. But it is necessary to show how Luther was body and soul a member of this class. For he was by no means a conscious agent of the petty bourgeoisie, he did not act mercenarily; rather he was convinced that the cause he fought for, even when he was advocating the extermination of the peasants, was a divine one, and that he was working for the spiritual and cultural welfare of human society. He was intellectually identified with the outlook of his class, considered its values as absolute and final, and was ready to sacrifice everything to them, in the present and in the future.

There is an essential difference between Luther's outlook and that of the humanists in general. The social position of the greater number of humanists in Germany was different from that of Luther, for while he was attached closely to a territorial prince, they lived mainly in the free imperial cities, or depended for their livelihood on ecclesiastical endowments or benefactors. Their most distinguished representatives, Erasmus and Mutianus—Erasmus I class among the German humanists for convenience sake, since he was considered by them their leader and passed a great portion of his life in Germany—lived on endowments, and thus were dependent on the privileged established class; their outlook is, for this reason, more dispassionate, yet more critical, than that of their contemporaries. Their criticism of contemporary society and thought is more searching and more inexorable than that of others; but at the same time they shrink more than the rest from proposing methods of reform which would imply violence or the disturbing of the aristocratic culture which they represented. They condemned in the strongest terms the demagogy of Luther. Other humanists, like Wimpheling, who were attached to the active life of the cities, were not so afraid of the advance of the rising class, and tried to use Luther's demagogy to further their own values.[1] At the same time, these men had not the trust in the human reason of an Erasmus or a Mutianus, and were not so free of dogmatism and traditional methods of thought.

Between Luther and the humanists there was then

[1] Cf. Wimpheling's advice to Maximilian in 1518 as to what attitude the Emperor should take with regard to Luther. The two groups within the humanist ranks are defined broadly by Janssen, *Geschichte des deutschen Volkes.* . . . Vol. I, but the difference between them is defined purely psychologically.

a certain social antagonism. In the intellectual sphere this antagonism crystallised into an irreconcilable controversy concerning the nature of man's reason. Erasmus and Mutianus, without any intention of a violent reform, could let their reason range freely over all questions, hoping that abuses would disappear with the gradual enlightenment of the class in authority, and in particular of the clergy. Luther, on the other hand, while seeing certain abuses as clearly as they, as a result of his advocacy of a violent reform had to provide a basis whereby the reform could be held in check when it had reached a certain point. He had to obviate the possibility of an anarchy such as the uncontrolled use of reason threatened to cause. Thus he took his stand on certain dogmatic statements which ensured the establishment of another authority to take the place of the old one he intended to destroy. This dogma he found in the doctrine of Christianity as expounded by St. Paul in the Epistle to the Romans. It enabled him to overthrow the Church as he found it and to establish his own. Humanists such as Erasmus opposed him because he was acting contrary to the spirit of Christ in rousing mass passions, and because he was reinstating a dogma. In particular, Erasmus was concerned with the dogma of the enslavement of man's will and the evilness of man's nature. He himself based all his hope of human advance on the infiltration of reason among men and on the feeling of personal responsibility. How, he asked Luther, can a good God damn men eternally for no fault of their own?[1] Luther's answer we know.[2] It was of essential importance for him to keep the masses, whose consciences he had raised above the authority of the Church, under the sway of some principle that should be beyond debate. There is no relationship between God's righteousness and man's; reason cannot inspect the decrees of God, but is itself naturally inclined towards evil; man's corporal part is bound, therefore, to accept unconditionally the existing order.[3]

The normal definition of the distinction between the humanists and Luther is that the former concentrated on the improvement of this life, while Luther wished merely to restore the true faith. This is Luther's own definition, expressed most concisely when he calls Erasmus an " epicurean " and himself a theologian. But we must not accept so superficial a definition. The humanists saw the essence of religion in Christ's command " Love one another," and attempted to make everyday life a part of religious observance; and, as has been seen, Luther's conception of the true religion included the establishment of a strict moral code. This meant, of course, an entirely different attitude towards things of the world. The humanists turned their critical minds on all beliefs which prevented

[1] Erasmus, *De libero arbitrio*, 1525.

[2] *De servo arbitrio* (Vol. XVIII); cf. Chap. II.

[3] The closing sentences of *De servo arbitrio* show the irreconcilableness of Luther's and humanistic principles—" In this book I have not merely advanced problems, but have laid down firm theses . . . to no one do I allow a judgment on them, but advise everyone to accept them " (Vol. XVIII).

the development of the reason and which were designed to come between man and man; especially on the common superstitions, whether they were consciously nurtured by the Church or not. Luther, on the other hand, who showed great acumen in discovering the origin of ecclesiastical superstitions, suffered other beliefs which favoured authoritarianism in general to remain. Thus he believed in the personal existence of the devil, and had many a hand-to-hand struggle with him. He believed absolutely in the supernatural elements of the Bible and in its literal truth, being centuries away from the allegorical interpretation given to the biblical myths by Erasmus and Mutianus. He believed that portents still presaged important occurrences— " This way of God's, to let nothing great occur without portents, was well known to the Jews from their own experience," etc. He believed the legend of the finding of two fabulous figures, the " pope-ass " in 1496 at Rome, and the " monk-calf " at Freiburg, and said that such figures could not have been created by men, but must be the handiwork of God. He believed in the existence and power of witches, though at the end of his life he said that since the introduction of the true faith the number of witches had grown considerably less, this conclusion being due possibly to his change of circumstance.[1]

[1] Christian Thomasius, one of the first thinkers in Lutheran lands to break away from Lutheran orthodoxy, said in 1701 that Lutheran like Catholic divines had encouraged the belief in witchcraft and other superstitions because they found such a mental attitude of great use to them.

To test all fact in the light of the reason was, then, not the aim of Luther. His aim was the establishment of a new authority, not the modification of the old. Thus the bland satire which is the characteristic of the works of Erasmus is completely absent from Luther's writings. He is hasty, passionate, extreme. He enjoyed violent controversy, was no respecter of persons, and in his invective outvied his most ready-tongued adversaries. But it must not be thought that he only destroyed culture and was the antithesis of humanism. For long he was, indeed, on good terms with several of the German humanists, and shared the common admiration of Erasmus, whom he quoted in his commentaries. Some of his closest followers, and notably Melanchthon, could be reckoned among the band of humanists. Though he rejected the culture of the schoolmen, he repeatedly praised that of his good burghers, and feared for its destruction. Some historians have even claimed that only through him were the acquisitions of humanism transferred to the mass of the people. We must examine his attitude to the arts and to education.

To appreciate correctly Luther's attitude towards culture we must take into account not only what he personally admired, but also what he refused to destroy. Thus, he himself had no great feeling for pictorial beauty. He wandered through Rome, when sent there on his mission in 1512, without noticing the works of art which were the passion of the humanists of his day; he was blind to the excellences of the new painting and of the remnants of classical sculpture and architecture. All that he praised in Italian painting was the exactitude with which natural objects were portrayed. This is the only criterion he knew, "to counterfeit." But he was by no means iconoclastic towards painting. He would not allow sacred pictures to be adored, but he approved of them as mementos of sacred events. He even recommended that men should fill their houses with pictures illustrating sacred subjects so that they would be perpetually reminded of God's presence and power. He recognised the quality of evocation in pictorial art, and highly praised such artists as Dürer and the elder Cranach. He differed, however, from the humanists and such Renaissance artists as Dürer in that his judgments were not measured by any idea of " perfection," by any classical ideal, but by a moral standard.

His lack of appreciation for pictorial art was more than made up for by his devotion to music. Music, he said, is " a lovely and splendid gift of God, and near to theology "; and once, after hearing several motets and songs, he exclaimed: " Since our Lord God has cast such noble gifts into this life, which is, in spite of all, a sheer dung-heap, what will be our lot in that eternal life, where everything will become most perfect and joyful? . . ." [1] He treasured music particularly as a consolation in distress; in his depressed moments he often had recourse to the lute he played and the melodies he loved. He says:

[1] *Tischgespräche*, 1538, December 17.

" Music is the best solace to a troubled mind, for by
it is peace and refreshment restored to the heart. . . .
It chases away the spirit of sadness." He loved it
most for its effect on the passions: " Music is a half-
discipline and corrective, for it makes men more
sweet-tempered, and gentle, more law-abiding and
reasonable " ; " it chases away the devil and makes
the people joyful; it makes one to forget all wrath,
unchastity, pride, and other vices," etc. Luther
justified the joy which music brought him by an
interpretation within the scheme of his theology: he
says several times that music is next to theology
among the gifts of God. But he did not make it a
condition of good music that the musician should be
animated by a moral intention. He was as apprecia-
tive of the beauty of secular songs, and of songs on
the subject of the Virgin, the content of which he
considered repugnant, as of that of the hymns and
psalms he most approved. He would recite old
German songs with relish. To whatever end it was
adapted, music was for him a gift of God, and it was
man's duty to tend it. So he rebuked those nobles
at the Saxon Court who had persuaded the Elector
to disband his musicians. " Kings, princes, and
lords must encourage music ; for it is fitting that great
potentates and regents should rule over good free
arts and laws . . . one reads in the Bible that pious
kings instituted, kept, and rewarded men and women
singers." Music was, then, for Luther a free art
which should be used to embellish this " dung-heap "
of a world. Because he scorned the world, he did

not scorn certain of God's gifts. He did not examine
the logicality of his attitude, but merely showed
himself determined to save here, as elsewhere, certain elements of the culture of his times.[1] In particular, of course, he wished to turn this gift to the
service of the extension of God's kingdom on earth,
and he recommended that no schoolmaster, and no
priest, should be without practice in music. The
Lutheran Church, barren in most arts, has achieved
a peculiar perfection in music.

While in his devotion to music Luther was in
agreement with all the cultured classes of his time,
in another respect he differed from the humanists
and the majority of his learned and cultured contemporaries. This was in his love and appreciation
of the vernacular tongue. The cult of Latin was
common to the humanists, as to the theologians of
the day. In the latter case it was the effect of
traditionalism in thought and outlook. The arid
controversies in which they consumed themselves
had no existence outside the traditional concepts
forged in Latin by the Fathers of the Church. They
did not dare to submit them to the test of translation
into an active, used language. Luther, too, in his
more abstract works, found it necessary to use the
Latin tongue. And its analytic terminology was
beyond comparison richer than any vernacular.
The humanists used a different Latin, and for a

[1] The Enthusiasts, on the other hand, wished to abolish
music. All æstheticism, as the product of a leisured class, was
bound to be repugnant to them.

different reason. They aimed at elegance of style, formal distinction, *eloquentia*. They imitated classical authors, in particular those distinguished for stylistic qualities. But their admiration of Latin authors was not the result of a chance fashion. In them they found a moral attitude expressed, which seemed to them an ideal. Instead of the aridity of contemporary theologians, or the coarseness and passionateness of popular writers, they found in them dignity and elevation. The care with which their favourite authors—Cicero, Vergil, Lucian, etc.—fashioned phrases and epigrams indicated a detachedness from vulgar interests which seemed to the humanists to indicate moral exaltedness. It seemed necessary to them, when composing, to detach themselves from the actuality round them; this resulted on the one hand in absurdly exaggerated, stilted conceits, but on the other in the bland acute satire of an Erasmus, which was so much more telling for its apparent disinterestedness.

Luther also admired classical authors. He was fond of quoting tags from Vergil, Ovid, Plautus, and showed that he understood the value of a well-turned expression. But chiefly he admired them for their moral value, and ranked them according to a didactic standard. He never showed any understanding for, or sympathy with, stylistic elegance or with the moral attitude it represented. His purely doctrinal writings were written in the dog-Latin of the medieval theologians; the method, form, and the conceits with which he worked were those of the school which was the scorn of the humanists. And when he engaged in controversy in Latin, the tone he adopted was the opposite of bland satire. It was always a matter for him of saving souls from impending destruction and society from disruption, and Luther sustained all his controversies in a spirit of passionate earnestness which very often exploded into vituperation. The responsible position he held amid the clashing social antagonisms of his time, the knowledge that his decisions decided the movement of masses, made the detached, æsthetic attitude of the impotent—and voluntarily impotent—humanists impossible to him

Luther's obduracy towards the attractions of *eloquentia* was not, however, due to a lack of feeling for the beauties of language. He found his delight not in the dead tongue, but in a living one; not in the organ of a learned society, but in the social medium of the people he lived amongst. With the advent of printed books the cult of the vernacular was spreading among writers towards the end of the fifteenth century. Many translations were made; medieval folk-books like the Siegfried legend, epics like the Roman de Reynart, chivalrous tales like *La belle Melusine*, were re-written or translated for the consumption of the new reading public, which was in the main the middle class—it remained a point of honour in certain aristocratic circles to read and possess only manuscript books.[1] The common

[1] The Elector Frederick of Saxony, for instance, being especially delighted with Luther's work *On Secular Government*, had a manuscript copy made of it for himself.

demand for literature in German developed an interest in the vernacular among the learned. Thus in 1483 the Vulgate was translated into German and printed. Sebastian Brant, who had some claims to be called a humanist, wrote in German his *Ship of Fools*, an imitation of medieval satire. Geiler of Kaisersberg, a priest of considerable classical learning, preached German sermons in which he showed a great appreciation of the nature of German words and idioms, bringing his points home by playing upon words. Thomas Murner, a close contemporary of Luther's, who engaged in bitter controversy with the reformer, broke away from theological custom by writing polemical works in German, and in particular enriched his language with expressions chosen from trades and occupations. But Luther surpassed all these men not only in his conscious furthering of the German tongue, but also in his appreciation of its peculiar qualities and in his manipulation of it. He would note down the idiomatic expressions used by strangers calling at his house, and the different dialects of Germany. He delighted in technical expressions, in the everyday household language of his neighbours, and was the decided enemy of artificial Latinised German.

The most choice example of Luther's style is his translation of the Bible. Here he was free to devote himself to style without polemical distractions. His main principle of translation is that it is not enough to translate words from the Hebrew or Greek into German, but it is necessary to translate Hebrew and

Greek phrases into German phrases. The translation of the Vulgate of 1483 follows the former inadequate method, Luther follows the latter, and it is most instructive to compare the two.[1] Instead of the awkward Latinised German of the former, Luther uses an imaged, idiomatic language which has all the characteristics of a living tongue. He is not afraid to remodel whole sentences of his original, and he uses all the resources of German syntax. In his hymns he employs the same method. He was fond of quoting old German ballads and poems, and he uses their metaphors and constructions in his own work. Thus his hymns are nearer the folk-song than the cultured poetry of his period; they have a vigour of image and rhythm which sets them far above the pedantic prosaisms of the master-singers. His general prose-writings show the same characteristics. Written mainly in great haste, and in general of a polemical tone, they are unequal in style. But where he is most hasty he is often most striking, using every-day idiomatic phrases which remain in the memory. His coarsest invective has a flavour and character about it which put a personality and a society vividly before us.

But Luther did not merely use the German language. He was conscious of its peculiar genius. There are to be observed in certain thinkers of this period the beginnings of an historical outlook on

[1] Characteristic examples of the two translations are quoted side by side in: *Deutsche Literatur. Reihe Reformation*, Vol. I, pp. 292 ff.

cultural phenomena. Certain of the humanists took a revolutionary view of the Bible by comparing the literature of the Jews with that of the Greeks and Romans, the Hebrew mythology with the Greek; [1] others pursued this line of thought further when they compared the German heroes and history with classical, a development which served nationalistic passions and interests.[2] From this latter charge Luther is by no means free, but the tendency led to a most fruitful investigation into the differences between the Latin and the German tongues. The immediate occasion of Luther's most pregnant work on this subject, the *Missive concerning Translation*,[3] was the complaint of many people that his translation of the Bible was not close enough to the original. Luther answers the various charges in a masterly way. An example will show his method and principle. It had been complained that in translating Romans iii. 28—*arbitramur, hominem justificari ex fide absque operibus* (we conclude that a man is justified by faith without the deeds of the law)—Luther had added the word " only " when there was no " *sola* " in the Latin version—" we hold that a man is justified *only* by faith, without the deeds of the law."

[1] Cf. Lorenzo Valla, Erasmus, Mutianus.

[2] Cf. Wimpheling's *Germania*, which served anti-French passions: Johann Aventin who proved that the Germans were descended from Trojan ancestors; Irenicus, who passionately defended the German character against the common charges levelled against it; Reuchlin himself, who proved that the Elector of Saxony was of Trojan descent. There were founded also at this time many historical and antiquarian societies with a strong patriotic bias.

[3] *Sendbrief vom Dolmetschen*, 1530, Vol. XXX, ii.

Luther answers: " It is true, these four letters, *sola*, do not stand in the Latin and Greek text; and the blockheads stare at them like cows in front of a new gate. But they do not see that the meaning of the text implies the word, and it belongs to it if one wants a clear and vivid German version. For I wanted to speak German, not Latin nor Greek. . . . And this is the nature of our German speech. When one speaks of two things, affirming the one and denying the other, there is need of the word ' only ' in company with the word ' not ' or ' none.' As when one says: ' The peasant brings no money, but only corn '; ' No, I have at present no money, but only corn '; ' I have only eaten, and not drunk '; and such-like innumerable examples out of daily usage. . . . For if I say: ' The peasant brings corn and no money,' the word ' no money ' does not ring so clear and full. . . ." [1] Luther takes other examples to show how " Latin words hinder us from speaking good German," and insists that the spoken German of his time must be the basis of translation and of writing in general. He is careful to say that where ideas or images of a special import occur which have no parallel in the German, it is necessary to break away from German usage; but in general his standard remains the imaged speech of every-day

[1] From an English translation, of course, the true force of Luther's analysis of German style cannot be estimated; as indeed I cannot show the excellence of his translation of the Bible to English readers; but this case has a sufficiently close analogy in the English language for me to risk putting it here. And in any case it shows Luther's method.

occupations: " one must go to the mothers in their homes, the children in the streets, the common man in the market, and look in their mouths to see how they speak." Besides writing a German which has not been surpassed, Luther laid down principles of literary composition which cannot be improved on.

These literary principles are based on moral considerations. Luther's expressed aim was simply to produce a language intelligible to the common man. But the cause of the vernacular against the classical tongues was not that of morality against culture. Luther could feel that his cult of the vernacular furthered the moral values he fought for; but he took also an immediate delight in the German language. He enjoyed to the full its constructions and its images; he wished to create a " fine, beautiful, praise-worthy German." His delight in language can be compared to his delight in music. His relationship to the humanists on this score was not that of a moralist to a group of lovers of beauty; but rather he opposed to the culture and beauty they admired another ideal of culture. His was narrower than theirs. His whole outlook was bounded by the restricted circumstances in which he lived; his thought scarcely transcended the boundaries of the electorate of Saxony, and was determined even more closely by his associations within Wittenberg and similar small towns. But his culture went forward and centred in a real, established community. The culture of the humanists went backward. It was based on a system already brought to crumbling point. They were collectors of the productions of the past, and, in spite of their humanitarian doctrines, sided with oppression rather than put their treasures, intellectual and material, into the rough, careless hands of a less cultivated class. Most of all they feared for that freedom of intellectual investigation which the laxity of the existing theocracy made possible. An enlightened intelligence like Erasmus had to revolt against a belief that this world was a " muck-heap," seeing that such a belief would include a repudiation of all earthly values, beauty, love, truth. Erasmus made the mistake of thinking that Luther was fighting a purely philosophical battle. But Luther was fighting primarily a political and economic battle. He ignored some of the intellectual progress made, and opposed other parts of it; but he helped to establish a community which could determine its own values. Human talents were for him gifts of God still, values within the muck-heap, put here to beautify and improve life. And though, by his dogmatic theology, he forbade men to apply their reason to religious and philosophical problems, his extension of the definition of the concept " secular " to the whole sphere of human activity outside faith led to the liberation of the reason with regard to human problems and institutions, and ultimately to the infinite development of the scientific spirit.

The favourable attitude of Luther towards the most advanced cultural ideals of his time, those of the humanists, can be clearly seen in his educational schemes. Education was one of his chief preoccupations from the beginning of his reforms. It was necessary for him to get hold of the youth of the country in order to train them in his way, and the task soon became urgent because of the dissolution of the monasteries and convents, formerly the chief places of education. He as much feared uneducated as wrongly educated men.

In *To the Christian Nobility* Luther first outlined a scheme of reform for schools and universities. But though it was chiefly the nobility who inherited the wealth of the ecclesiastical foundations, they did not proceed to any regulation of the institutions which had depended on the Church. Schools were neglected in Wittenberg itself. Teachers were not paid, nor was a curriculum fixed. In 1523 Luther proceeded to the reformation of the Wittenberg school, and in the following year he published his plan for the establishment and upkeep of schools in all Lutheran lands. It was addressed not to the nobility, but to the town-councillors: *To the Councillors of all German Towns, concerning the Institution and Upkeep of Christian Schools.*[1] He had to defeat these obstacles to his wishes: the avarice of the authorities who confiscated property without recognising their new social responsibilities; the narrowness of the citizens who wanted their children to receive a purely technical education; the demagogy of certain

[1] *An die Ratherren aller Städte deutsches Lands, dass sie christliche Schulen aufrichten und halten sollen*, 1524, Vol. XV. Actually the town-councillors of Leisnig had already been a particular stumbling-block in the way of his social reforms in the preceding year; cf. p. 215.

religious teachers who said learning was more hindrance than help to a Christian life. He says, the moment is particularly apt for action. Money is there ready to be used, from the confiscation of Church property; peculiarly gifted men are there, with a high opinion of their calling, *i.e.* his own band of reformers; take advantage of this momentary grace of God and institute schools to save the young from harm. The best wealth of towns is " fine, learned, reasonable, honourable citizens." Education has two aims. First, it should profit the Gospel and the Church. For this end the ancient tongues should be studied. It is true, says Luther, since the Holy Scriptures have been so well translated a priest ignorant of Latin and Greek may preach Christ's Gospel; but in order thoroughly to expound the Scriptures and to refute false doctrine, one needs more than a knowledge of the translation, and the sermons of these ignorant preachers are in the main " unsound and weak." Learning may not be necessary for piety, but it is necessary for the refutation of error. This remained Luther's constant view-point; it meant that the control of dogma was always in the hands of a learned body of theologians.[1] In the second place, education should profit the secular order, "so that it should not become a wild, unreasonable body." The ancients put us to shame, for, without any knowledge of the true Gospel, they had

[1] Luther says, it is all very well to be inspired: he himself was inspired as much as anyone. But he needed learning and a close knowledge of the Greek and Latin texts of the Bible in order to overcome the Papists and establish the true faith.

admirable social institutions and brought up their children wisely. Luther gives evidence of a purely secular ambition: "Let us also use our reason for once . . . so we also shall contribute something to the improvement of the world." Even if the soul did not exist it would be necessary to have learned and skilful statesmen, councillors, and the like. Languages should be studied by those destined for secular office, for besides their religious use they are an honour and a delight in themselves, a "fine and noble gift of God." Luther expresses his scorn of those "beasts and wild animals" who scorn intellectual delights.

Besides languages—by which Luther means, of course, Latin, Greek, and if possible Hebrew—history, music, and mathematics should be studied. These studies are but child's play, says Luther, compared with the "devilish muck" of the philosophers and sophists which he himself had been forced to study, and yet they produce clever and able men. Libraries should be founded, as had been done in the monasteries; but the treasures of the latter, the works of the School and Philosophers, in particular of Aristotle, should be thrown on the rubbish heap. In the new libraries there should be the Holy Scriptures in Latin, Greek, Hebrew, and German; the best Commentaries, and the Fathers of the Church, in all languages; such books as are useful for learning languages, the Poets and Orators, whether they are pagan or Christian; books on the fine arts and on all crafts; books on medicine and law, though here great care is needed in the choice—it can easily be seen why certain legal commentaries were dangerous for the Lutheran cause; and lastly, chronicles and histories should be collected, no matter in what tongue they are written, for they are " of wondrous use, to tell the way of the world and how to govern; yea, also, to show God's wonders and works." Luther shows himself eager to collect and profit by all the best knowledge and art of the past. He does not want the children to be overladen with knowledge, however, nor to be made into fine lords. Boys should be sent to school for an hour or two, and spend the rest of the day at home, learning their trade; girls also can well spend an hour in the school. All these arrangements he recommends to the municipal bodies. The nobility had shown itself unfit; and parents were unfit to look after the education of their children for three reasons: some are unnatural, and " like ostriches " take no care for their offspring's welfare; some are ignorant and have learnt only to provide for their bellies; the rest are too busy at their trade or in their homes to spare time for the children. It is thus necessary for the municipalities to provide schools and salaried teachers.

As a consequence of this appeal of Luther's, schools were endowed and opened in various centres—at Magdeburg, Nürnberg, Eisleben, for instance—and under able teachers reached an efficiency comparable to the former humanistic schools which were always the admiration of Luther.

But for some time their fortunes were subject to fluctuations. The matter of endowment was the chief difficulty, and the contentions which arose on this account are well illustrated by the events at Leisnig in 1523. Luther had here attempted to found a model community on the principle of the voluntary responsibility of all for the welfare of the whole. Articles were drawn up for the disposition of the confiscated Church property; each member was to have part control, and regular contributions were to be made out of the general fund out of which the salaries of priests and teachers were to be paid, together with all school expenses. But the town-council, in whose hands the confiscated property was put in trust, hampered the working of the scheme from the first. They did not wish to give up enough money for the planned works, and most were abandoned. Luther, in great vexation, urged the Elector of Saxony to force the town-council to yield up the necessary endowment, but the Elector was, of course, loath to exert pressure on his most settled and reliable subjects, the ruling class of the towns.[1] So the whole matter fell through. Such a situation threatened in all places where Luther's reforms were carried through. In small towns, especially, where there was no tradition of learning and culture, there was bound to be considerable opposition to expendi-

[1] At times Luther expressed his approval of the action of the common body of citizens who forced the town-councils to support public works—a further expression of class feeling. Cf. Preface to *Predigt, dass man Kinder zur Schule halten solle,* Vol. XXX, ii, p. 520. But Luther preferred action on the part of the ruler to this democratic method.

ture of wealth for such objects, and it was exactly in such towns that pietism and other movements which considered learning as harmful to true piety took root. In the large towns, on the other hand, excellent schools were founded and maintained.

Luther had not defined any particular system of teaching, and in this matter great confusion arose. In their ardour for the reforms, teachers tended to throw over with the subjects also the methods of the monastic schools, and to count rather too much on the influence of the divine spirit to make good their lack of method. Luther took steps to put this right in the general visitation of Lutheran communities organised in 1527. In the *Instruction of Visitors* [1] he outlines a method to be followed in the schools. Only Latin shall be taught, not German or Greek or Hebrew, which burden the children too much. The school must first be divided into classes. In the first class shall be grouped the children who are learning to read. Children's text-books with the alphabet, the Lord's Prayer, the Creed, and other such prayers shall be first used. When they have mastered this, they shall be given Donatus to read, and Cato to be expounded: the schoolmaster shall expound a line or two one hour, and make the children repeat it later. They shall learn to write. Every evening they shall be given a number of Latin words to learn. The next class is for the children who can read and who must learn grammar. In the afternoon the teacher shall expound to them some of

[1] *Unterricht der Visitatoren an die Pfarrherrn*, Vol. XXVI.

those which prove the value of education in strengthening the existing order. But he assumes two
axioms which were even then questioned by many.
The first one lies in the religious sphere, and is, that
learning is necessary to preach Christian doctrine;
subjoined to this, that a class of priests is in accordance with Christ's teaching. The second is one of
politics. Luther assumes that secular organisation,
which prevents the individual from becoming a
wild beast, is necessarily the existing order of his
time, and that any attack on this is equivalent to
anarchy; that existing law is the expression of wisdom and not of force. Luther passes over these
assumptions in order to proceed ruthlessly to the
affirmation of his system of education, of a priest-
class, and of the existing order. We can see, therefore, how closely allied was his cultural to his
religious and political attitude; after breaking down
what was specifically the organ of another class,
another society, he affirmed absolutely the values of
his own class. A learned organisation, cut off from
its economic origin, had been one of the main
strengths of the ecclesiastical state; after a new state
had been formed, representing predominantly aristocratic and petty-bourgeois interests, such an organisation could be used as a main strut of the new society.

The reform of University education was carried
out on the same lines as that of the schools. Luther
did not propose any fundamental change, the
University being still for him a place for the production of theologians, jurists, and doctors of medicine.

He was passionately opposed to the rationalism of Aristotle's thought, and so the *Physics*, *Metaphysics*, and *Ethics* of Aristotle were banished from the Universities, though his *Rhetoric* and *Poetics* remained.[1] Canon law was done away with, the Bible being considered enough to decide on ecclesiastical and religious sin. Luther advocated the abolition of the Roman law because of its subtlety, and says: " Reasonable rulers together with the Holy Scriptures should be enough "; but since men do not allow themselves to be ruled by the decisions of theologians, and as good rulers are rare birds, he says the native law of the land and the traditional customs should be considered authoritative, with as short a form of law-suit as possible. In this matter, however, he had to give way to the will of the rulers, to whose advantage the Roman law was. The method of teaching he recommends is that of argument with the teacher. He supports University education with the same reasons as he had used for elementary education; to make a good citizen of one's child was as categorical a command as to make him a Christian.

Even if Luther, the dogmatic theologian, did not

[1] Actually the dogmatism of Lutheran theology developed a repetition of medieval scholasticism in the Universities; and with this the cult of Aristotle revived. Thomasius (*fl.* 1700) states that at one time in the orthodox Lutheran University of Leipzig the doctors had to take an oath of faith in Aristotle. Thomasius himself fought passionately against the authority of Aristotle in moral and political thought, and conjured up the memory of Luther in his aid. It goes without saying that in the Lutheran University, as in the medieval, the theologians were predominant.

stand on so high a cultural plane as Erasmus, the opponent of prejudice, yet his cultural ideals and his system of education represent a great advance on those of the great majority of contemporary churchmen. His schools were in the tradition of the best schools of his time, those of Deventer and Magdeburg, for instance, and though his Universities were bound to become centres of reactionary pedantry, it was not his intention that normal cultured citizens should pass through them.[1] The deterioration of culture which actually took place after the Reformation had affirmed itself has been wrongly put down to Luther's influence and will. It was the destruction of the conditions under which the Renaissance had come to blossom that caused its withering. The most enlightened thought of Erasmus and Mutianus, as of Lorenzo Valla and Leonardo in Italy, had to remain fragmentary and unfulfilled because of its danger for contemporary society. It flourished on the basis of a careless ecclesiastical aristocracy; but when this basis was called into question, and in some places destroyed, the Roman Church showed itself even more bitter against the humanists than the Lutherans. From the beginning the papists identified (though wrongly) Erasmus with the Lutheran cause, and as the two opposing theological doctrines and religious systems crystallised out, Erasmus found himself contemned and attacked equally by both. A scientific, rationalistic attitude towards

[1] See Paul Kalkoff " Stellung der deutschen Humanisten zur Reformation," in *Zeitschrift für Kirchengeschichte*, Vol. XLVI.

philosophical problems was forbidden by both sets of dogma; but the Lutheran thought, because of its liberation of the secular sphere from the control of religious thought, gave a greater opportunity for the development of natural science—though demanding that lip-service to religion which has been the characteristic of so many scientists who have pondered on the philosophical basis of their work. Leibniz is a characteristic example of the Protestant scientist.

A glance at the economic and political conditions under which Luther tried to carry out his cultural reforms will make clear the inevitability of the retrogression. One has only to read the account of Germany given by Æneas Silvius, later Pope Pius II, to realise the barbarity of the German princes who affirmed with the Reformation their leadership of Germany. Luther himself had hard work to find among them princes whose piety and culture he could praise, and amongst the rare names he praises we find that of Georg of Frönsberg, the imperial general who sacked Rome! Such rulers would sacrifice only with the most extreme reluctance any of the wealth they gained from the confiscation of ecclesiastical property, and thus many of the charitable and educational institutions of the papal Church were deprived of their endowments. In the case of schools, Luther was able to rally enough support from the citizens in the towns to re-endow those which were left destitute, or to found new ones. Burghers could see fairly clearly the advantages which accrued to their children from education, and besides that, they could control very closely the schools in their locality. With Universities it was different. A University education does not redound so clearly to the benefit of the locality in which the University is placed, and its control passes out of the hands of its founders into that of the Senate. Thus the Universities suffered most severely from the Reformation. Whatever old endowments were left to them became of increasingly smaller value owing to the general rise in prices during the sixteenth century. At Erfurt, whose University had been most flourishing before the Reformation, the professors tried to carry on by existing on their lecture fees, which had formerly been devoted to feasts. The fees had to be raised. The number of students consequently dropped. And in 1530 Luther complained that the University at Erfurt was lying desolate. Such causes were out of Luther's control; and it was to such causes that the apparent retrogression of culture was largely due. At the same time, the scope of the schools was increased so as to take from the Universities their junior students. It is in the schools such as that inaugurated in 1526 by Melanchthon in Nürnberg that the real achievement of Luther's cultural ideals lies, and these schools were well in the forefront of the educational methods and theory of the time.

CHAPTER VIII

CONCLUSION

In the face of the contradictions in Luther's theology and ecclesiastical policy, theologians have had to advance " excuses " for these inconsistencies. In particular, psychological explanations have been put forward to the effect that Luther was a man of a certain temperament, or was not able to foresee later developments, later interpretations of his doctrine. This would be all very well if Luther had not been the leader of a large and conscious movement, or if his thought and activity in other spheres belied the contradictions in his theology. It has been the purpose of this book, however, to show how Luther kept himself at the head of the reform movement, and how contradictions analogous to those in his theology appear in the rest of his thought. He destroys the authority of the Ecumenical Council and erects the Consistory, condemning the independence of thought of an Erasmus; he proclaims the integrity of the secular order and supports the princes in their struggle against the supreme secular head; he states that the commands of law have no divine quality, and yet promises that even heavenly rewards will follow on their observance; he knows that the princes are immoral and unreliable, yet puts in their hands, unreservedly, the material and spiritual welfare of the people; he opposes and accepts usury. With all this he shows himself to have been a man of great courage, perspicacity, integrity; these qualities distinguished him from his fellow-believers like Melanchthon and Bugenhagen, who were on many occasions ready to serve expediency when Luther insisted on principle. These contradictions cannot be overlooked. They cannot be ascribed to Luther's temperament or to his inadequacy to the task the times set him. The principle underlying them is fundamental to Luther's whole historical importance. This principle is not logical, it is not psychological; the repeated conflicts of Luther's life show it to have been sociological. The consistency amid all these contradictions, the consistency *of* the contradictions, is the consistency of class interest.

There are perhaps many people who are ready to grant that Luther's thought was guided into its peculiar lines by sociological moments, but who would not agree that the interest of any one class dominated his decisions. They might claim that he worked for the welfare of the German nation as a whole. If we examine his theory and practice in any one isolated sphere, this claim might seem persuasive. When Luther attacked the Papacy he was speaking for the whole of Germany; when he opposed the levellers and religious communists, the princes, nobles, and middle class united with him;

when he finally sanctioned the struggle against the Emperor, most classes were with him; when he called for control of the financiers and monopolists, as when he scourged the morals of the princes, he represented a great body of opinion. Such was the constitution of society at that time, as it was shortly analysed in Chapter I of this book, that any of these causes could count on the support of several classes. When we consider Luther's whole work, however, what is important is the highest common factor in the various bodies or groups who profited by his pronouncements. As far as practical action goes, there are two groups whose interests were continually advanced by Luther—the secular princes and that part of the middle class which had authority in the cities and the guilds but was not engaged in foreign monopoly trade or in finance. These two groups had by no means identical interests, but had common enemies, and each was a condition of the prosperity, of the existence, of the other. In England and France the alliance between the two had already shown itself to be the most powerful political force in society as it was then constituted. Owing to the strength of the territorial princes and the peculiar structure of the Empire, such a development had not been possible in Germany; the Emperor was not powerful enough to impose his will on the princes, nor had a constitutional monarchy as proposed by Nicolas of Cusa any reality. The consolidation of the absolutism of the princes, on the other hand, could not proceed in so simple a manner as that of the kings of England

and France, for legally they were subject to the Emperor. The establishment of their independence needed a fundamental revision of the theory of society, so that while in England and France the growth of the monarchy meant in actual fact a continual gradual encroachment on the powers and rights of the Church, in Germany the theory of the Church, its theology, its political and legal theory, had to be revised in order to sanction such encroachment. This is the reason why Germany was the battle-ground of the Reformation, why the theoretical controversy there replaces the political struggle elsewhere as the focus of interest, why Luther is the German counterpart of Henry the Seventh or Louis the Eleventh.

Sanctions are not, of course, the affair of an all-powerful executive; its wishes are sufficient reason for its actions. Sanctions, which are simply the reverse of safeguards, are the affair of those who fear the power of others, whose desires have continually to be restrained by social necessity and who thus develop a theory of society and law to guarantee their own prosperity. Thus Frederick the Wise could remain a pious Catholic while placidly continuing with the expropriation of ecclesiastical property, and the bitter struggles of conscience were reserved to Luther and his associates. But Frederick and Philip of Hesse and all the other Protestant princes could not have acted as they did without the sanction and approval of the mass of the people. Although they possessed the most effective executive power in the Holy Roman Empire, they could use it only subject to the consent of the main body of their people, or to that, at least, of the authoritative leaders of the middle classes such as the town-councils. For instance, they more than once objected to taxes, which the Emperor Maximilian wished to impose, on the grounds that their subjects refused to pay and threatened rebellion. It was from these classes that the princes drew their power. Though their interests often clashed, they could both gain most from an alliance and a mutually favourable compromise. Thus the princes sustained Luther in his theological controversy as well as in his struggle with the Papacy as a temporal power and a Church. The complete revision of the social theory which this entailed gave them the support of all law-abiding citizens and contributed to their mutual advantage. Those princes who, on the other hand, claimed merely a reform of the Catholic Church, gained very little in comparison, and in particular could not later make their loss good for lack of a social theory which would justify such acts as expropriation of ecclesiastical property and centralisation.[1] A comparison between Frederick the Great and the Emperor Joseph the Second illustrates this, even so long after the Reformation as the end of the eighteenth

[1] Of course the victory gained by the Protestant princes redounded to the benefit of Catholic princes too. The overthrow of medieval authority was general. The position of the Catholic princes became as absolute as that of the Protestant, except that formally the Church was an antagonistic force in Catholic principalities. Even the Jesuits avoided attacks on the established secular powers.

century. The alliance between princes and middle class against the rest of the groups of interest in Germany was, then, no mere expediential matter, but a re-moulding of society and of its theoretical bases. Thus it is natural that Luther, who fashioned the shape social theory took in certain lands and preserved for three centuries, should have felt himself serving high ethical causes rather than the interests of a part of the middle class.

It is the necessary result of class conflict that the struggle is carried on in the ethical sphere as well as in that of politics. Where masses are engaged it is necessary that they should believe that certain guarantees accompany any alliance they make. And since, up till quite recent times, teleological guarantees were thought most binding, the struggle is waged over metaphysical as well as ethical issues. The pretended absoluteness of the resultant systems is the counterpart of the wish for the perpetuation of the respective political systems. Thus at any time there are a number of ethical systems, all differing and all claiming to be correct, all corresponding to the interests of particular political groups. An analysis of society according to the economic interest of several groups, such as was attempted in Chapter I of this book, is rightly considered inadequate, for a description of society does not assume resemblance to reality until groups are classified according to their ethic, to their general outlook on moral problems. Similarly, we cannot say definitely that Luther was the representative of the interests of a certain class until we have defined the moral outlook of this class and have proved Luther's to have been identical with it.

We can see in all ages that social classes produce an ethical system, or at least moral principles, which justify their economic and political rôle. The pious burghers of Muggleton, "mingling a zealous advocacy of Christian principles with a devoted attachment to commercial rights," are the rule, not the exception. This principle held in Luther's time as now, and the various social groups can be classified quite clearly according to their ethics. We need hardly consider the case of the Catholic Church in this connexion, since it defined itself primarily as a metaphysical and ethical system; it is enough to say that this system was developing into the rationalisation of the needs of the Papacy as a secular empire, with a supreme dogma of the infallibility of the Pope. All parties in Germany outside the Church opposed the imperialist policy of the Church and the principle of the identification of the secular and the spiritual worlds, but within this united opposition ideas as to what was right and wrong were varied. The concept of class gains in clarity if the various outlooks are described.

Among the Imperial knights, the remnants of the old fighting forces of the Empire, the idea of faithfulness to tradition and to the Emperor predominated. All the new developments in society were dangerous to them. Their property was expropriated by the larger secular princes. Their military services were no longer valuable in an age of mercenary armies and heavy artillery. The rise in prices which hit the peasants so heavily harmed them equally, for they lived on peasant labour. If they pledged their lands, they had no method of meeting their obligations, and were continually brought to penury. From a military point of view they were no match, even when they combined—a difficult matter, since their lands lay scattered all over Germany—for the armies of the princes, or for the forces organised by the larger cities. There was no independent career open to their younger sons, unless they became submissive courtiers at the court of a more powerful prince. It was natural that they should look back with longing on the times when they formed an integral part of the Empire, and that among them the concept of the "good old times" was current. Ulrich von Hutten was their spokesman. The virtues he praised were nationalism, loyalty, freedom. The Emperor was the national hero, in spite of many clear proofs that Charles V, even Maximilian, were first and foremost dynasts interested chiefly in the glorification of their own house. Simplicity of life was a virtue in Hutten's eyes, and luxury meant for him the unpatriotic consumption of foreign goods, delicacies from the Orient, from France, and Italy. Trading he considered not merely a dishonourable, but also a dishonest and immoral calling, and said that the robber-knights were justified in waylaying the merchant caravans both for moral and practical reasons. The courts of princes were in his eyes hotbeds of luxury, the court officials sycophantic and lacking in the prime virtues of independence and honesty. His moral code is, indeed, convincing up to a point, and we can understand why he championed Luther, and why Luther felt in many things akin to him.

The international bankers and merchants also developed their moral code, which was not very different from that of Big Business to-day. A feeling of responsibility towards commercial and social obligations, which was quite lacking in Hutten, is their basic principle. There is a noteworthy letter written by Jakob Fugger to Charles V (received by the Emperor on April 24, 1523) [1] in which this belief in the sacredness of a business obligation leads the financier to use the most outspoken language to his Emperor, language which would have seemed most presumptuous in any contemporary. Loyalty and honesty belonged naturally to the code of such a man. The class to which the Fugger belonged subscribed to more specifically Christian virtues, as their counterparts do to-day. That is, they exploited the community by all the commercial and financial tricks possible, and had no hesitation in stimulating wars, but joined with this a strong local patriotism and made charitable endowments on a large scale. While they could not be devoted allies of the Papacy, their peculiar enemies were the knights and the secular princes, who were not wealthy enough to

---

[1] Quoted by Ehrenberg, *Capital and Finance in the Age of the Renaissance*, p. 80.

give them room for operating and who put all sorts of barriers in the way of commerce. Thus on the whole they were loyalists, since the rule of the Emperor was the best guarantee for freedom of operation, though in this matter they were bound to be determined by particular business ties.

When we come to the broader masses of the middle class a different outlook appears. The moral code of the Imperial knights could be so clear because as a class their social function was clearly distinct from that of any other contemporary class, and they had a definite attitude towards contemporary society as a whole. The middle classes, on the other hand, affirmed social forms as they were, merely demanding modifications. In their morality, therefore, they dealt with individual failings and the duties of small groups, principles whereby society could be made more efficient from their point of view. In particular, the idea of work came to have a peculiar value. The general attack on the Catholic Church was delivered on the ground of the unproductivity of the institutions of the Church. There was immense moral indignation against the begging orders of friars, against begging of any sort, and one of the first tasks in towns which accepted the Reformation was not merely the organisation of charity, but the provision of employment for the unemployed. The two aspects of this principle of work—the obligation to work and the right to a proper reward for work—arose from two different social attitudes within the middle classes, as we shall see in a moment.

The main body of social satire and criticism rose from these classes, and was based on this idea of the moral value of work. One of the most popular works of the times was a modernised version of the medieval French epic of *Reynard the Fox*, in which efficiency is extolled at the expense of virtue. The famous *Ship of Fools* of Sebastian Brant satirises vices (follies as he significantly calls them) chiefly from the point of view of efficiency. Thus the parasitic Church, drunkenness, debauchery, idleness, unproductive professions like the law, come in for their full share of blame. But the idea of efficiency is not an abstract moral idea; it applies to a particular social form and is a form of propaganda for an existing order. Thus we find at this time a general satire by the citizens in the towns of the peasants, of their stupidity, avarice, even poverty; but the town-councils did not support the reasonable demands of the peasants put forward in the Twelve Articles, and acquiesced in their further suppression after the failure of the Peasants' Revolt. The peasants' conception of the proper conditions of work, of efficiency, was not shared by the town-dwellers. The limitations of middle-class ethic is shown most evidently in a passage in the *Ship of Fools* where Brant reproves those journeymen who, by working too much, cause over-production and break prices, so that the masters suffer: [1] he does not, however, criticise guild monopolies and control of price and production. On the whole, this moral

[1] Seb. Brant. *Narrenschiff*. *Ein gesellen schiff*.

236

outlook is based on the obligation to work; and the Christian virtues of love and submissiveness are adduced to sustain this system amongst those who do not profit by it. It is the outlook of a privileged class. In its attack on the privileges of the Church it needed some dogmatic authority which would guarantee its own privileges. Thus it upheld the idea of authority; and in the free Imperial cities the oligarchic despotism of the patriciate, which followed on the Reformation, was equivalent to the despotism of the princes in the principalities. The sharp distinction drawn by Luther between the secular and spiritual sphere corresponded exactly to the needs of this privileged class. This theory justified privilege in the secular sphere, while freeing from its burden in the spiritual. Luther satisfied them, further, in that he attempted to dissuade from violence, which always means mob-rule, and to reform by the unanimous wish of the people, *i.e.* through existent authority. " Passive resistance " and the belief in the necessary victory of the true doctrine became articles of their moral code.

But not all of the middle classes profited by privilege, and not all subscribed to this moral code and the metaphysics on which it was based. Amongst those groups who suffered from ecclesiastical and secular privilege the idea of equality had subsisted since the introduction of Christianity. The principle of equality of conscience, which Luther enunciated as a polemical weapon, rallied round him the lower classes in the towns, and also the peasants. But workers in industry like the weaving, which was largely controlled by big merchants, and journeymen, for whom entry into the mastership was hindered by artificial restrictions, imagined that equality of conscience meant a real freedom for them. On one side they attempted to reorganise the Church on an equalitarian basis, each member taking the lead as the spirit moved him; on the other, their inspirations led them to devote themselves to the religious life, in which none took precedence of them, and to prophesy awful punishments to those who still were occupied with earthly business and self-advancement. They instituted common ownership of property, and put expropriated ecclesiastical property to the service of the whole community. Their principles were love and charity towards their neighbours and devotion above all to the life of the soul. But where they encountered the resistance and hard-heartedness of other classes they did not merely prophesy judgments from God. They found biblical texts enough, and inspirations enough, to justify the use of armed force against their unbelieving oppressors. Their aim became the immediate realisation of the kingdom of Christ, and their moral code embraced both mortification of individual desires and the unhesitating sacrifice of their lives. It was apparent to them, under Münzer's guidance, that while their doctrines were held by only a section of the community there could be no question of Christ's kingdom on earth. It was only later, after the cruel lessons at Mülhausen, Münster, and other places, that their doctrines took the idealistic form of pietism.

The peasants form the last group of interest we have to consider. Owing to the savage exploitation to which they were subject, their rising was of a more frankly economic nature than the movement of any other class. The anti-clericalism in the Twelve Articles is fairly obviously due to economic causes. But no peasants' rising during the Middle Ages had been free of communistic elements. The peasants had promised to retract any of the Twelve Articles which could not be justified by Christ's teaching, and in Christ's teaching they found many elements of agrarian communism. Equality of conscience meant for them equality of property, and they held a belief in the viciousness of towns and town occupations. It was this class-consciousness which led to the powerful uprising which threatened the princes themselves, not merely the economic demands peculiar to the situation of the peasants at that time.

In the organism of Germany at the beginning of the sixteenth century these were then the moral components, corresponding to the economic components. Any individual in any of these groups could consider himself working for the furtherance of high moral values and could justify antagonism against any other group on moral grounds. And moral principles, inculcated by education and environment, are as potent to move men to action and self-sacrifice as is economic advantage; further, being necessarily more vague and general than

239

economic principles, they can unite together masses which have not necessarily the same ultimate aims. This was the strength of Luther's cause. By fighting the Papacy on metaphysical grounds he began at the right end of the stick. He rallied the whole of Germany, even foreign countries, on his side. From this beginning his doctrines narrow themselves down, repudiating alliances which had earlier been expedient. But though here and there his political and economic theory shows what class he represents, the struggle is mainly on a moral and theological level. He is convinced that he is protecting the Good and True. The analysis of his theology has shown, I hope, that the new elements in it were only such as allowed a new social order to be formed. His morality is everywhere marked with the standards of a particular class. His moral strictures on the peasants and enthusiasts bear in particular a class character. But the same signs are to be observed in his more general attitude. In his polemics against the levellers, as against the Turks, he stresses above all the danger threatened by these enemies of society to the family. He represents them as breaking up the home, sullying the purity of wives and maidens. Similarly, to describe religious experience he uses terms culled from the intimacy of family life. He believed that in the family the highest Christian virtues are cultivated, and wished to make it the model for the State. But the family is more than the fundament of the moral order: it was the basis of the state in which he lived. The preservation of the family is essentially linked up with the preservation and inheritance of private property. The enthusiasts and peasants were, of course, in the main quite innocent of the crimes against women which Luther imputed to them; but he was right in diagnosing their economic levelling theories as a threat to the family. It was a natural step to transpose the argument to the moral sphere. And the mass of supporters which followed Luther would not be misled by this method of attack, but rightly inflamed more hotly thereby.

There is no need to repeat Luther's values. He shared those of the settled, authoritarian middle class—the belief in "passive resistance," in the inevitable and pacific victory of the truth, in authoritarian methods, in the family, in Christian love and submissiveness, in the sanctity and necessity of work. Though he worked quite clearly for his own class in the economic sphere, he certainly had no consciousness of the class basis of these moral values. For this reason he was so dogmatic in maintaining them; Melanchthon, who was a finer and more rational mind, was led to waver this way and that through too rational an approach to Luther's dogmas. It must not be thought, of course, that this whole system was the abstract product of the middle class, simply and solely the rationalisation of the economic needs of the contemporaries of Luther. The metaphysical system, especially particular concepts, of such a class might be imagined

241

in a different form than Lutheranism. They evolved, however, historically from a former state of society, together with the middle class itself. They are modifications of ideas and values which permeated the whole of society, and at no point in history is a complete revision of concepts possible unless a complete revolution in authority is aimed at. Luther's class enjoyed some part of authority before the Reformation, however, and consequently did not wish for a complete revolution. Indeed, it needed to sustain some authority in order to maintain its privileges against the claims of other classes. Thus Luther worked inside the traditional framework of ideas, and even preserved the traditional concept of dogma.

An analysis of a historical period such as this book attempts is, of course, inadequate without a wide perspective into the preceding and following times. Every aspect of the civilisation at a particular epoch arises from and is determined by the past. The materialistic conception of history must be distinguished from the crude theory that historical events are determined by economic conditions. The vital fact arising from the effect of economic moments on human beings is the creation of social and political forms, of class; and understanding of the nature of class is a presupposition for the understanding of history. The warring classes of the past, in competition for the hegemony of society, have created systems of metaphysics, of ethics, an art of their own. The idealism of individuals has contributed to the self-preservation, the self-assertion of the class. It is a complex task to penetrate to the heart of so elaborate a structure. It is hoped, however, that this book has not neglected any important aspect of the problem, and provides a clue to the meaning of the immense fermentation which was the Reformation.

BIBLIOGRAPHY

In general I have relied on the many histories of the period of the Reformation for my material. For a more detailed list of sources and histories see J. S. Schapiro, *Social Reform and the Reformation*, and Georges de Lagarde, *Recherches sur l'esprit politique de la Réforme*.

Apart from the general literature of the period the following contemporary works have a particular bearing on this book:

D. Erasmus. *Enchiridion militis christiani*, London, 1544.

”   *Colloquia selecta*, with an English translation. London, 1749.

”   *Adagia.*

”   *Moriæ encomium.* London, 1709.

”   *De libero arbitrio.* . . . Basel, 1524.

Rufus Conradus Mutianus. *Der Briefwechsel des C. Mutianus (Geschichtsquellen der Provinz Sachsen*, 18). Halle, 1890.

J. Wimpheling. *Germania.* Strassburg, 1885.

Ulrich von Hutten. *Gespräche.* Leipzig, 1860.

Hutten and Crotus Rubeanus (with others). *Epistolæ obscurorum virorum.* London, 1909.

Lucas Rem. *Tagebuch.* Augsburg, 1861.

Götz von Berlichingen. *Lebensbeschreibung.* Nürnberg, 1731.

Sebastian Brant. *Das Narrenschiff*, ed. Goedeke. Leipzig, 1872.

Aleander. *Die Depeschen des Nuntius Aleander vom Wormser Reichstag* 1521, *übersetzt und erläutert*, von Paul Kalkoff. (*Schriften des Vereins für Kirchengesch.*, 17.) Halle, 1886.

Otto Clemen. *Flugschriften aus der Reformationszeit.*

Joh. Eberlin von Güntzburg. *Werke in Neudrucke deutscher Litteraturwerke des 16ten und 17ten Jahrhunderts.* Nos. 139–141, 170–172, 183–188.

Thomas Münzer. *Ausgetrückte Emplössung.* . . . Mülhausen, 1524.

”   *Hochverursachte Schutzrede.* Mülhausen, 1524.

Kayser Sigismund's " Reformation aller Stände des Heiligen Römischen Reichs." Printed in Goldast, *Collectio Constitutionum Imperialium*, 1713, Vol. IV.

BIBLIOGRAPHY

W. Böhm. *Friedrich Reisers Reformation des Kaisers Sigismund.* Leipzig, 1876.
Martin Luther. *Werke.* Weimar, 1883–1930.
" *Briefwechsel,* ed. Enders. Frankfurt am Main, 1884–95.

HISTORICAL WORKS

J. Köstlin und Kawerau. *Luthers Leben und Werke.* 2 vols. Berlin, 1903.
H. Grisar. *Luther.* 3 vols. Freiburg, 1911.
F. H. S. Denifle. *Luther und Luthertum in der ersten Entwicklung quellenmässig dargestellt.* Mainz, 1904.
H. Boehmer. *Luther in the Light of Modern Research.* London, 1930.
J. Binder. *Luthers Staatsauffassung (Beiträge zur Philosophie der deutschen Idealismus,* 13). Erfurt, 1924.
Otto Harnack. *Lehrbuch der Dogmengeschichte.* Tübingen, 1910.
Ernst Troeltsch. *Soziallehren der christlichen Kirchen.* Tübingen, 1912.
F. von Bezold. *Geschichte der deutschen Reformation.* Berlin, 1886.
L. von Ranke. *Deutsche Geschichte im Zeitalter der Reformation.* Berlin, 1839–47.
" *Die römischen Päpste, ihre Kirche und ihr Staat im 16ten und 17ten Jahrhundert.* Berlin, 1834–36.
J. Janssen. *Geschichte des deutschen Volks seit dem Ausgang des Mittelalters.* Freiburg im Breisgau, 1897.
K. Lamprecht. *Deutsche Geschichte.* Berlin, 1891–1907.
L. Pastor. *Geschichte der Päpste seit dem Ausgange des Mittelalters.* 1891–1895.
Ludwig Geiger. *Renaissance und Humanismus in Italien und Deutschland.* Berlin, 1882.
W. Dilthey. *Weltanschauung und Analyse des Menschen seit der Renaissance.* Berlin, 1914.
Paul Kalkoff. *Humanismus und Reformation in Erfurt, 1500–1530.* Halle, 1926.
" *Ulrich von Hutten und die Reformation (Quellen und Forschungen zur Reformationsgesch.,* 4). Leipzig, 1920.
" " *Stellung der deutschen Humanisten zur Reformation*" (*Zeitschr. für Kirchengesch.,* Vol. XXVI).

245

BIBLIOGRAPHY

K. Burdach. *Reformation und Humanismus in Italien und Deutschland.*
J. N. Figgis. *From Gerson to Grotius.* 1911.
R. H. Tawney. *Religion and the Rise of Capitalism.* 1930.
Georges de Lagarde. *L'Esprit politique de la Réforme.* Paris, 1926.
Max Weber. *The Protestant Ethic and the Spirit of Capitalism.* London, 1930.
J. S. Schapiro. *Social Reform and the Reformation* (Columbia University Studies in History and Economics, Vol. XXXIV). 1909.
W. Sombart. *Der moderne Capitalismus.* Leipzig, 1922.
H. Hauser. *Les Débuts du capitalisme.* Paris, 1930.
Sir William Ashley. *An Introduction to English Economic History and Theory.* 1888.
R. Ehrenberg. *Capital and Finance in the Age of the Renaissance* (*Das Zeitalter der Fugger*). London, 1928.
K. Lamprecht. " Zum Verständnis der wirtschaftlichen und sozialen Wandlungen in Deutschland vom 14ten zum 16ten Jahrhundert " (*Ztschr. für Sozial und Wirtschaftsgesch.*, Vol. I).
R. Zöllner. *Zur Vorgeschichte des Bauernkrieges.* Dresden, 1872.
W. Zimmermann. *Allgemeine Geschichte des grossen Bauernkrieges.* Stuttgart, 1854.
E. Walther—Thomas Münzer. Paris, 1927.
O. Merx—Münzer and Pfeiffer. 1889.
K. Kautsky. *Communism in Central Europe in the Time of the Reformation.* London, 1897.
Max. Neumann. *Geschichte des Wuchers in Deutschland.* 1865.
H. Wiskemann. *Darstellung der in Deutschland zur Zeit der Reformation herrschenden nationalökonomischen Ansichten*, 1861.
B. Duhr. *Geschichte der Jesuiten in den Ländern deutscher Zunge.* Freiburg im Breisgau, 1913.